To Florence:

THE LONG DARK WALK

BY JOHN OLSZEWSKI

John Olszewski

© 2019 John Olszewski.

ISBN: 978-0-7404-7749-2 (Paperback)
ISBN: 978-0-7404-7747-1 (Hardcover)

Published by
Higginson Book Company
Salem, Massachusetts

www.HigginsonBooks.com

This book is dedicated to the memories of all the victims of the murderers discussed in it. May they never be forgotten.

"There are a thousand hacking at the branches of evil to one who is striking at the root."

Henry David Thoreau

PROLOGUE

If you are reading this, it is safe to assume that the act of murder and or murderers fascinate you. But have you ever asked yourself why? Looking into oneself is never an easy thing, but I felt that was the approach I wanted to take, as well as describing my experiences with my subjects and what if anything I learned from them.

If you expect to just see page after page of letters reprinted or hear fantastic tales of how the killers got into my head, you won't find that here. I am not out to make money off the notoriety of my subjects even though they are the main draw.

Most of the individuals I will talk about are ones that I corresponded with through the mail. A couple I exchanged emails with and others I obtained some of their letters written to other people. As of this writing the totals stand at one hundred five while accumulating six hundred ninety six letters and twenty seven emails. I have also spoken on the phone with some, attended court hearings of others, and lastly met and interacted with others in person from my time working in the correctional system bringing my total subjects up to one hundred sixteen.

Along with my personal accounts with the subjects I will give you significant background information on them that played a part in them becoming what they are. Those background contributing factors will include: family history/genetic indicators, homosexual tendencies, MacDonald triad indicators, which are bed wetting, cruelty to animals, and fire setting, the three behaviors can suggest sociopathy. The remaining factors are medical issues, mental health issues, military service, paroled to kill again, physical abuse, sexual abuse, and substance abuse. We will discuss their significance in the conclusion.

Serial killers were the main focus of my study, with seventy four of my one hundred sixteen subjects fitting into that category, but over the years it expanded to include: mass killers, (eight), professional athletes, (ten), serial rapists, (four), and spree killers, (three), along with a few other high profile killers, (eighteen). There are subcategories of these as well that I will mention. Those are angels of death, cannibals, and team killers under serial killers and family annihilators, school shooters, and workplace shooters under mass killers and spree killers. Other subcategories you will see mentioned are cult killers and teen killers.

Some killers I believe I really established a friendship with, others I believe tried to use me for resources. Some killers I will spend a lot of time on, others I will only briefly mention, all depending on how much contact we had. Throughout this book I will be honest and not hold back. I may occasionally make a diagnosis, which I do feel qualified to do.

With all of that being said, I feel ready to begin, and invite you to take The Long Dark Walk with me.

John Olszewski

> "Evil lurks in places you would never imagine and tries to charm its way into your life."
>
> Unknown

I.

The origins of my journey can be traced back to my high school years when I began working at the Salem Public Library. It was there that I found myself drawn to the true crime section. I fondly remember hiding in the stacks and devouring books on serial killers Ted Bundy and John Wayne Gacy while my mind formulated a litany of questions with a need to be answered.

As I started college the need was still there and I wasn't doing anything to appease it. I knew I had to make a change. So I did. After two years in college majoring in Urban Forestry I switched colleges and started an Associate's Degree in Criminal Justice where I was educated by local law enforcement personnel.

Some questions may have been answered during this time, but more arose. I felt I believed in the death penalty in these early years with the exception of serial killers who I felt suffered from mental illness and couldn't control their actions.

Learning about the McNaughton Rule then troubled me even without the psychology background yet. If you are not familiar with this legal test for insanity, it is what defines who is sane and who isn't. If you knew what you were doing was wrong, you are sane. If you didn't, you are insane. I will return to this in a future chapter that details my psychology background.

It was the Fall of 1994 now. I was nearing graduation when a defining moment occurred to motivate me into action. Earlier in the year the state of Illinois executed John Gacy who fascinated me to no end. I often joked to others how I wanted to write to him which was met with criticism.

I hoped my early education had me on the path to a career working with them. I figured there are others for me to work with even though John Gacy was out of the picture. The world was intrigued by Jeffrey Dahmer now, the serial killer star of the decade. Unfortunately his reign was short lived as he was murdered at the Columbia Correctional Institution by Christopher Scarver on November 28th at the age of thirty four. I vividly remember walking out of a class in college as the students cheered the news.

Pressure arose in me to write to a serial killer now, for I felt their numbers to be declining at an alarming rate. This of course was not true, merely my subconscious convincing me to do it.

So, I did it. I wrote…I waited…and I received in December, my first response. It was from serial killer Arthur Shawcross.

"She was giving me oral sex, and she got carried away...so I choked her."
Arthur Shawcross

II.

I am not sure why I chose Arthur Shawcross, but I did. I had read Misbegotten Son by Jack Olsen while working at the library. He was certainly an interesting case, a former Army veteran who killed two young children and was paroled after nearly fifteen years only to graduate to the murdering of women. He stated he had multiple head injuries and was sexually abused by family members as a boy. He also was a bedwetter and a fire setter. Then he claimed he experienced trauma while in the military. An abnormality in his brain was even used during the trial as well as his XYY syndrome and antisocial personality disorder. Experts tested his IQ at one hundred seven at this time. He took the chance to acknowledge cannibalism and was suspected of necrophilia as well.

His first letter seemed friendly enough, but it soon became evident he was clearly hamming it up for the pen and paper and much of what he said seemed exaggerated, putting his childhood abuse and military exploit claims into question.

Over our time corresponding he sent me three poems: I, Serials, and Wisdom. The titles are very revealing and clearly validify his enjoyment of being a celebrity. He also sent me an index card with his fingerprint and a disturbing quote. Years later I found multiple cards like this, some with the exact same quote, being sold on online murderabilia sites. He had apparently cornered the market.

Murderabilia was growing quickly at this time with paintings by John Gacy reaching a thousand dollars plus. Seeing this, Arthur began doing his own, color by number however.

Some background to give here is explaining that murderabilia is anything related to a crime or criminal sold for profit. At this time Ebay was even allowing the sale of such artifacts. Years before this New York created a "Son of Sam" law, aptly named after serial killer David Berkowitz, which prohibited an inmate from profiting off the notoriety of his/her crime. Although many inmates had found ways around this law. Giving it as gifts to friends, who sold it for them, then giving the inmate a gift in return. Each state needed to come up with such a law on its own, and many had not.

Needless to say his selling of artwork caused controversy as it found its way into displays at art galleries. Due to immense pressure from victim advocates Ebay finally banned the sale of murderabilia.

When asked on his view on the death penalty, Arthur would say, "Let us just say that if New York State had a death penalty, I would not have done what I did!".

Our correspondence went from December 1994 until March 1996 accumulating sixteen letters. Arthur died in prison on November 10th in 2008 at the age of sixty three from cardiac arrest.

But before our correspondence had ended, I had begun my second and third correspondences.

"You don't understand me. You are not expected to. You are not capable of it. I am beyond your experience."

Richard Ramirez

III.

In the early stages of this twenty year plus journey I was batting with a perfect average as my second and third attempts were both answered. First by William Heirens and then by Richard Ramirez.

William Heirens, "The Lipstick Killer", was a serial killer who was historic in many ways. The University of Chicago student became one of the first criminals to bare the moniker, "crime of the century". He also became the longest tenured inmate in Illinois Department Of Corrections history as he spent over sixty years incarcerated after being convicted of three murders.

He also became the first killer I questioned the court's decision on. He confessed to three murders, but after controversial interrogation techniques that are no longer allowed. Over the years many people petitioned for a retrial, etc, but none would ever be given.

Personally I regret not signing a petition. We lost touch due to his health.

Our correspondence went from September 1995 until October 2004 accumulating thirty five letters. William died in prison on March 5th in 2012 at the age of eighty three from complications of diabetes.

Richard Ramirez, "The Night Stalker", was a serial killer who was Latino and convicted of thirteen murders and basked in it. He came from a tough childhood having a history of head injuries, physical abuse at the hands of his father, and witnessing his close cousin Mike fatally shoot his wife. After that Richard got heavily into drugs contracting hepatitis C along the way. He is probably the most famous killer I ever corresponded with to this day.

His trial cost one million eight hundred thousand dollars, the most in California history up to that time.

From him I also received my first pieces of art done by a killer. One piece in particular is one of my two most valued pieces I have ever received.

It was of a deceased woman in bed, naked and covered only from waist down. There were slashes across the throat and breasts. The piece was done in black and red ink. Most of Richard's work was childlike and not really good. This piece however was better by far, then anything I have ever seen by him.

During this time I took a non-credit course on handwriting analysis. I did this with the hope of getting an even better insight into my subject's mind. The most notable thing I saw repeatedly with his artwork was his signature. He would sign his name Richard Ramirez and under it, his moniker, "The Night Stalker".

His name was always written half the size of his moniker, which experts would agree means he was inadequate as himself, but very confident as "The Night Stalker".

Richard also became the first inmate to ask me for things. Almost every letter asked for pictures of women. He also had many other pen pals and once accidently mailed the wrong letter to me. One of those pen pals, Doreen Lioy, he married in 1996.

There really wasn't much substance to his letters which were always brief yet often written on personalized stationary. He did mail me a copy of Philip Carlo's book on him, The Night Stalker however, promising to sign it, which he forgot to.

Our correspondence went from June 1996 until February 2002 accumulating thirty nine letters. Richard died in prison on June 7th in 2013 at the age of fifty three from complications secondary to B-cell lymphoma.

Now the floodgates were opened and new pen pals came fast and furious.

"The dead won't bother you, it's the living you have to worry about."
John Wayne Gacy

IV.

Around this time I began to make acquaintances with other people who wrote to killers, true crime authors, and even met the famous F.B.I. criminal profilers John Douglas and Robert Ressler. Robert Ressler was the man who coined the term serial killer.

From these connections I was able to obtain three letters written by John Wayne Gacy. One from April 1990 to Sondra London, one from January 1993 to Harold Nalven, and one from January 1994 to Kregg Sanders. He had personalized stationary, his with the heading: "Execute Justice...Not People."

Not as revealing as I hoped, they still showed a cunning side to him, as he negotiates deals for his artwork and talks about his media image.

John was a homosexual with an IQ of one hundred eighteen who suffered from seizures as a child and an antisocial personality disorder after enduring physical abuse by his alcoholic father. He had graduated Northwestern Business College before forming a substance abuse problem during the course of murdering thirty three young boys for which he was found guilty of. While in prison he was stabbed by serial killer Henry Brisbon on February 15th in 1983 but survived only to be executed on May 10th in 1994 at the age of fifty two by lethal injection.

His last meal consisted of Kentucky Fried Chicken, a dozen fried shrimp, french fries, fresh strawberries, and a can of Diet Coke. His last words were: "Kiss my ass." In 2012 John's nephew Raymond Kasper was convicted of sexual assault.

By now I had also begun my Bachelor's Degree in Behavioral Science, making sure to take any electives concerning abnormal psychology or crime available. I was devouring all the knowledge I could, completing Salem Citizens' Police Academy at the same time as well.

I was learning of all the different subcategories of serial killers and the differences between serial, mass, and spree killers. I also took any chance I could get to discuss the subject with others who were interested.

I should probably take the time here to explain the differences between the killers and their subcategories that I focused on.

Serial killers are defined by the F.B.I. as an individual who kills three or more, usually, but not always, in multiple locations, with a cooling off period between the murders. Mass killers are defined as an individual who kills three or more in one location, with no cooling off period. A spree killer kills three or more in multiple locations with no cooling off period.

As for the subcategories: Angels of death are usually employed in hospitals and kill people under their care. Family annihilators kill at least two of their immediate family members often in a mass event. School shooters commit mass killings on school grounds. Team and teen killers are self-explanatory.

Is it possible for a killer to fall into more than one of these categories? Absolutely. Ted Bundy was unique in so many ways, but the main reason was he morphed from a serial killer into a spree killer, not many people realize that. After his escape from prison he was on the run, no cooling off period.

"Mr. Maimoni has no chance of success on parole in his current state of pathologically lying."

Massachusetts State Parole Board's 2017 decision on 71 year old Thomas Maimoni.

V.

Thomas Maimoni was a local killer who was convicted of killing a woman. His correspondence with me was both unique and personal for many reasons. Ironically as I write this chapter I have just learned of his death in prison on October 18th in 2017 at the age seventy two.

As a resident of Salem, this murder captivated me. Tom and the victim both lived a short walk from my house. This case had it all and seemed a perfect fit for the Lifetime Movie Network.

The year was 1991 and I had just graduated high school and was enjoying my summer before starting college. The victim, a middle aged married woman went missing, reports indicated she was last seen with Tom and heading out on his sailboat. He denied these claims.

Police suspected him, but had nothing to go on until a local lobsterman pulling up his traps was shocked to find a body weighed down by an anchor caught in his trap.

Tom went on the run and soon Unsolved Mysteries was featuring a story on him.

Eventually he was apprehended near the Canadian border. His lies would begin or continue in full force now.

A local author, Margaret Press, wrote a book on him a few years later, Counterpoint. Upon it's release I met her at a book signing and had an in depth discussion on him. I wrote him in July of 1996 and received one response.

From my point of view this was a once in a lifetime insight into the mind of a narcissist. It is impossible to describe all the knowledge he credited himself with, as well as groups he was in that depended on him. So unfortunately he didn't have time for a correspondence with me.

This led me to contemplate a controversial approach for me to take. I needed to know how he would react if a woman wrote him. It is something I struggled with and feel a great deal of guilt about today, but I made the decision to write Tom as a woman. It is an approach I would use a couple more times in the future but I would never garner a response like this again.

Up until now I had used my personal address, but with this change of approach I needed a new address. So around this time I obtained a post office box.

For every one letter I sent as a female it seemed I would receive five responses. I have never seen this level of obsession before. The bragging continued. I received personally made cards, journal entries, and even a manuscript to his novel of the events from that day.

His personality and lack of remorse led me to believe this wasn't his first murder, especially when other women came forward to state he tried to get them on his boat as well, and a few that did go, told tales of unwanted sexual advances.

I voiced this opinion to professionals and found they agreed. If he did or not, I felt he certainly would have again had he gotten away with this murder or paroled.

My second series of correspondences went from October of 1996 until September of 1998 accumulating sixty one letters.

I love to sum up Tom with this quote: "The exaggerated sense of your own self-importance is exhausting." - - -Jessica Strobietto

(Handmade Christmas card from Tom)

> "He told me that he told her he was going to kill her. He wanted to see what her argument would be for staying alive."

Roy Norris on Lawrence Bittaker's comments about the death of Andrea Hall.

VI.

Dayton Leroy Rogers, "The Molalla Forest Killer", is a serial killer who was convicted of the murders of seven women and would become the first subject to send me a personal photo of himself. I wrote him asking questions and opinions on a book written on him by Gary King called Blood Lust. He claimed it had many inaccuracies.

He refused to answer my questions but gave me a chance to continue corresponding, but on other subjects he pre-approved. His second letter was a litany of questions on my opinion on things. He was also surprised I would continue, however that second letter did not generate the answers he wanted.

Our correspondence went from December 1996 until April 1997 accumulating only those two letters.

Lawrence Bittaker is a serial killer who along with Roy Norris were convicted of five torture murders. He was adopted and had an IQ of one hundred thirty eight. He was intense and our exchanges had to meet his requirements or our correspondences would be terminated. I was routinely told my letters were not interesting and "need to improve". Occasionally I asked about other killers there at San Quentin State Prison and he either pretended not to know of them or wondered why I care about them when I'm writing him.

Clearly he wanted positive attention heaped on him and to be in the dominant role. Years later I would write his partner in murder, Roy Norris, who fit the mold of the submissive in their twisted partnership.

When I met John Douglas, the now retired F.B.I. profiler, he was doing a lecture before signing copies of his Mindhunter book. At some point during his lecture he started talking about Bittaker & Norris. He then played an audio recording of a woman being savagely tortured at their hands.

To hear that in person is very difficult, knowing it is real, and not just a movie. Listening to an adult revert back to a child and beg for their mother is something you will never forget.

Something correctional officers claim they will never forget is watching games of Bridge being played at San Quentin between serial killers Lawrence Bittaker, William Bonin, Douglas Clark, and Randy Kraft. The combined death tolls of these four men could easily exceed one hundred. With that kind of company Larry grew bored with me and stopped answering as he had promised to do.

Our correspondence went from November 1996 until September 1998 accumulating nineteen letters.

He was the first killer to give me attitude and I learned a lot from this and how to handle it in the future.

"Check, and mate. You never had a chance!"

Michael Ross in a letter sent to Dr. Stuart Grassian, a psychiatrist who had argued that Ross was not competent to waive appeal.

VII.

Michael Ross was a serial killer who was convicted of four murders, but admitted to eight, six in Connecticut, and two in New York. There is so much I can say about him that I could probably write a book on him.

First off I have to say he was probably the most intelligent subject I ever corresponded with. He was a graduate of Cornell University, an Ivy League institution. He had been physically and possibly sexually abused as a child and would become the first subject I would lose to an execution.

When I first started writing him he had started to switch over to a once a month newsletter due to the large number of people writing him. These letters would evolve into daily journaling and were often accompanied by copies of articles he wrote that had been published in numerous magazines and newspapers such as The Journal Of Psychiatry & Law.

I would still write him letters and he would answer or comment on certain things in the margins of the newsletters. The major point we agreed on was a separate facility to house serial killers so we can work with them and learn from them.

Genetics plays a major factor as Michael's mother had been institutionalized at one point and he also had an uncle who committed suicide. Michael himself had an anti-social personality disorder.

Michael did numerous interviews on death row which were incredibly insightful. He was honest and seemed desperate to understand why he did what he did. He would volunteer for any treatment available, but none seemed to help as he acknowledged being haunted by the twisted desires while incarcerated. They were so intense he fought the courts to move up his execution.

If I had been asked, I would have attended his execution, and I very much wanted to protest it. I did receive a goodbye and thank you letter from him for my support over the years. After his execution I would receive an invitation to a private burial in Connecticut.

His execution at the Osborn Correctional Institution on May 13th in 2005 at the age of forty five by lethal injection, was the first and only in New England still, since 1960. He did not request a special last meal and declined to make a last statement.

Our correspondence went from January 1997 to May 2005 accumulating seventy three letters, the most I would ever receive from one subject.

His execution backed my theory that the death penalty isn't a deterrent for most multiple murderers, as life has become too unbearable for them to handle.

> "I will in all probability be convicted, but I will not go away as a monster, but as a tragedy."
>
> Joel Rifkin

VIII.

Joel Rifkin is a serial killer who was convicted of murdering nine prostitutes. He would became the second killer I wrote as a woman.

Joel whose IQ was one hundred twenty nine had been adopted and suffered from dyslexia. His first job was a library page, same as me. He had studied at Nassau Community College, State University of New York-Brockport, and State University of New York-Farmingdale, but never completed a degree.

While in prison, and a few years before I would write him, Joel would be involved in a physical altercation with mass killer Colin Ferguson.

Unfortunately he did not wish to start a correspondence with me. He was however very polite about it and not obsessive like Thomas Maimoni was when I previously tried this approach. He also mentioned his involvement in a program to help women on the street.

Our correspondence was in February of 1997 accumulating one letter.

Bobby Joe Long was a serial killer who was convicted of murdering eight women. He was one of the most unpleasant killers I dealt with.

His childhood was filled with head injuries and an unusual relationship with his mother all while struggling with XXY syndrome.

His letters were filled with such anger. I had asked for his opinion on comments the late Dr. Joel Norris had made in one of his books, Serial Killers: The Growing Menace, and he responded with a colorful description of Dr. Norris that I would rather not repeat.

The unique thing about his letters was the neatness of the writing. It almost looked to have been written by a female. It was evident the writing was slow and not rushed, which didn't match the emotions he was exhibiting. Or did it? Could he be in that much control of his anger?

I tried to engage his emotions to continue the correspondence, but I was unsuccessful. I still wonder what further letters might have exposed.

Our correspondence went from August 1997 until September 1997 accumulating two letters. Bobby was executed on May 23rd in 2019 at the age of sixty five by lethal injection.

His last meal consisted of roast beef, bacon, french fries, and soda. He declined to make a last statement.

"If I gave a shit about the parents I wouldn't have killed the kid."
Clifford Olson

IX.

Clifford Olson was a serial killer from Canada who was convicted of eleven murders. He became my first subject to come from outside the United States. He was one of Canada's most notorious killers.

I would diagnose him as a narcissist along with Thomas Maimoni. He may not be on Tom's level, but he was up there.

The scary part about his narcissism was that he was able to obtain so much documents on himself. He would routinely send me prison psych reports which I have no idea how he would have access to that kind of information.

In a bizarre twist he created a psychological profile on himself which was very interesting, as was his obsession with Pamela Anderson whom he had at the top of his Christmas wish list.

Our correspondence went from October 1997 until February 1998 accumulating fifteen letters. Clifford died in prison on September 30th in 2011 at the age of seventy one from cancer.

Randall Woodfield, "The I-5 Killer", is a serial killer who was convicted of three murders but suspected of many more, as well as rapes. He was an antisocial personality disorder as well as a cheat at chess.

Randy prided himself on his talents. He had been drafted out of

Portland State in the 1974 NFL Draft by the Green Bay Packers in the seventeenth round with the four hundred twenty eighth pick, but was one of the final cuts in training camp which many experts believe was his trigger that set him off on his murder spree.

He routinely sent me pics of himself in the prison yard with friends, always with his shirt off showcasing his good physique. He also sent pics of leatherwork he created at the prison workshop, consisting of belts, keychains, and wallets. All were done really well. I did purchase a few pieces from him which I used all the time.

Eventually we engaged in a game of chess through the mail. I was wise enough to copy our game sheet each time before sending it back, and my caution paid off as I caught him re-doing the sheet and changing moves.

I received newsletters from him that the prison created periodically that named him as winning numerous chess and weight lifting competitions.

Our correspondence went from April 1998 until November 1999 accumulating twenty letters.

I probably didn't give him enough attention, as he like Richard Ramirez had numerous women pursuing him. He has married three times since his incarceration. One of the many women he corresponded with was Diane Downs who was also in prison. She had killed her daughter and attempted to kill her two other children.

"All of a sudden I realized that I had just done something that separated me from the human race and it was something that could never be undone. I realized that from that point on I could never be like normal people."

David Alan Gore

X.

Alfred Brown is a local mass killer and family annihilator who is Asian and was convicted of murdering his parents and sister. He was the first mass killer and first family annihilator I would write. He was only fifteen at the time of the crime and politely declined a correspondence without saying much.

Our correspondence was in June 1998 accumulating one letter.

By now I was deep into my psychology studies in college and realized that the McNaughton Rule was outdated. When this came into existence we were still drilling holes into people's head to let out evil spirits when they claimed they heard voices. We now know that is a mental illness, yet we don't hold mental illness for anything in the court of law. We are a society based on retribution as evidenced by the few not guilty by reason of insanity verdicts.

Compulsions control people. This is painfully evident in our war against opiate addiction. I always compare a serial killer to an addict for so many reasons. They can not stop. Their time between murders gets shorter and shorter. And they often get caught in the depressive cycle after a murder much like an addict after using. In my conclusion we again will revisit the why and then the how the serial killer is created. But for now, back to the killers.

David Alan Gore was a serial killer who along with his cousin Fred Waterfield were convicted of murdering six women. David used his job as an auxiliary sheriff's deputy to acquire victims.

We discussed Jennifer Furio's book, The Serial Killer Letters, which David was upset over. He claimed she lied to him and used him to get what she wanted, and that he never gave her permission to publish his letters.

David claimed the only family member he was close with was his father and that at one time he offered to help law enforcement by giving them his views and they weren't interested. He also talked about his two sons and trying to re-establish relations with them.

Our correspondence went from June 1999 until July 1999 accumulating two letters. David was executed on April 12th in 2012 at the age of fifty eight by lethal injection.

His last meal consisted of fried chicken, french fries, and butter pecan ice cream. His last words were: "I'm sorry. I've had remorse...I'm not the man I was back then. I don't fear death."

Before moving on to the next chapter I'd like to take a moment to answer a question many of you are probably wondering. People have always asked me what I would write in the initial letter that garnered all these responses. Honestly it would differ.

I guess I had to profile the individual first to know what approach would work. Most of the early letters I stated I was in college and was interested in the case etc. Obviously I used the female approach. The other approach I would use was one of interest in their artwork. They sense money and it would pretty much guarantee a response. With that said, let's move on.

Grave of the Brown Family

"Killing became the same thing as having sex."

Henry Lee Lucas

XI.

Roy Norris is a serial killer who along with Lawrence Bittaker were convicted of five torture murders. He would send me my first envelope art. I didn't realize it at the time, but this tends to be a major form of art by inmates, as most don't have the money for drawing paper.

Roy had been sexually abused in his youth before joining the Navy. He also had a history of drug use and a suicide attempt.

His writing was very feminine and we mainly discussed a recent book that had published correspondences of serial killers, which he was included in. He explained he felt deceived by the author and taken advantage of.

Our correspondence went from July 1999 until August 1999 accumulating two letters.

Harrison Graham is a serial killer who is African American and was convicted of seven murders. The first African American serial killer I would write, his letters were really interesting. Drugs played a major factor in his crimes as did his mental state. His defense stated he had a dissociative identity disorder.

His letters clearly showed some form of personality disorder. He would routinely start his sentences with: Harrison thinks, or Harrison did this, etc... Third person usage can be a sign of narcissism, but this clearly wasn't the case here. Another meaning is removed from reality.

That is backed up in a drawing he sent me done in pen. It was of a fish jumping out of the water. The water was wavy and the drawing is perhaps the weirdest thing I've seen. It looks sexual and also very disassociated. I feel it is the product of a schizophrenic person.

Our correspondence went from October 1999 until January 2000 accumulating four letters. It is my fault the correspondence didn't continue as I honestly didn't know how to communicate with him. With my education and experience now, I would be better equipped to understand him.

Henry Lee Lucas was a serial killer who was convicted of eleven murders, some of which he committed with fellow drifter Ottis Toole. His cousin was serial killer Bobby Joe Long. Henry's mother was a prostitute and his father died when he was thirteen. He had an antisocial personality disorder with a lower IQ of eighty nine and enjoyed engaging in necrophilia. Henry also lost an eye at age ten.

I wrote him as a woman and was surprised what I received. I had expected a crazed unintelligent ramble. The letters were decently written and appropriate considering I was a woman. He talked about the day he murdered his mother who had physically abused him. He described specifics of the murder in great detail, a crime for which he served ten years before being paroled.

He would go on to deny later murders and in fact became the only death row inmate Gov. George W. Bush would pardon, commuting his sentence to life.

Our correspondence went from November 1999 until February 2000 accumulating two letters. Henry died in prison on March 12th in 2001 at the age of sixty four from heart failure. Ottis died in prison on September 15th in 1996.

"We do whatever we enjoy doing. Whether it happens to be judged good or evil is a matter for others to decide."

Ian Brady

XII.

Jerome Brudos was a serial killer who was convicted of murdering four women. He was a schizophrenic that had been physically abused by his mother before joining the Army. He suffered from a severe form of foot and shoe fetishism. This fetish was the main objective for him even though he would engage in necrophilia with them as well.

I obtained a letter he wrote to a woman from December 1996 before I would write him as a woman. In his letter to her he went into great detail of his time in the military. Our correspondence went for four letters from February 2000 until April 2000. Jerome died in prison on March 28th in 2006 at the age of sixty seven from liver cancer.

Christa Pike is a female killer who was convicted of murdering another girl of similar age whom she thought was a rival for her boyfriend. She was the first female I would write. As a result of her crime she would become the youngest girl ever sentenced to death in the United States at the age of eighteen.

At her trial she stated years of physical and sexual abuse along with brain damage from her mother's drinking while she was pregnant predisposed her to violence.

I received my second piece of envelope art from her, and it was the most interesting piece I would ever receive. She somehow got her footprint on the envelope in a multi colored/speckled paint with just an open area in the middle for my mailing address.

Our correspondence went from March 2000 until August 2000 accumulating four letters.

Shortly after our correspondence ended Christa and another inmate, Natasha Cornett, who I would write at a later date, attempted to kill another inmate and Christa received a conviction of attempted first degree murder.

Ian Brady, one half of "The Moors Murderers", was a serial killer from England who along with Myra Hindley were convicted of three murders but suspected of more. He was said to have tortured animals and to have had an antisocial personality disorder.

During the time we wrote he was on a hunger strike and was being force fed intravenously. We discussed his love of tobacco and fishing as well as what U.S. states he had visited. He was nearing completion of his novel The Gates Of Janus at this time, and we discussed that as well.

Our correspondence lasted for five letters from June 2000 until November 2000. Ian died in prison on May 15th in 2017 at the age of seventy nine from restrictive pulmonary disease. Myra Hindley died in prison on November 15th in 2002 at the age of sixty from bronchial pneumonia.

As I started my correspondence with Ian I was completing my Bachelor's Degree in Behavioral Science. I now contemplated not only the next killer to write but the next path my educational background would head.

"I tried to tell my mother two or three times about this stuff and she just wouldn't believe me. I even wrote a confession one time and hid it, hoping that Dean would kill me because the thing was bothering me so bad. I gave the confession to my mother and told her if I was gone for a certain length of time to turn it in."

Elmer Wayne Henley

XIII.

I think this would be a good time to re-visit my death penalty stance upon having completed my Bachelor's Degree and gaining a few year's experience with my subjects, their cases, and the criminal justice system. My view had now changed to be against it for everyone.

One unique thing I learned in college that stuck with me through the years was that statistics indicate people's views on the death penalty are based on their education. The higher the education, the higher the percentage of those against. I learned this after I had changed my view and it made sense to me.

By now I had seen first hand too many examples of it applied unfairly and mitigating circumstances such as those I listed in the prologue not taken seriously enough when deciding the verdict.

Mind you this is just one man's opinion, but I do feel confident in my opinion.

Elmer Wayne Henley is a serial killer who along with David Owen Brooks and Dean Corll, "The Candy Man", were convicted of murdering twenty eight boys whom they had lured to Dean's house with alcohol and drugs. He was a seventeen year old homosexual who had been physically abused by his alcoholic father. Their crimes came to light when Elmer killed Dean Corll, then called the police.

I wrote under the premise of acquiring his artwork. It was better than most of his fellow serial killer artists. Unfortunately I would never acquire any as they were a bit too pricey for me, and the fact I was torn over the ethics debate of helping them profit off the notoriety of their crimes. In the past, and future, I usually only helped with postage and fees to maintain our correspondence. There were a few exceptions however, like the purchases I made from Randall Woodfield which were items I needed, and not luxury purchases. At least that was my way to rationalize it.

He would give me his mother's phone number to contact her as she had most of his art. I would never call her however. Elmer loved the fact I worked in a library and stated science fiction was his favorite reads.

Our correspondence went from September 2000 until November 2000 accumulating three letters. I would also obtain a fourth letter he wrote to a man back in March of 1995 that was dealing his art for him. He thanked him for selling a vampire piece . He also talked about being in college.

"We agreed that if we had to pick five people in our class who would never, ever be accused as some type of mass murderer, Randy would be one of the five."

Former classmate and student body president Clarence Haynes on Randy Kraft.

XIV.

Randy Kraft, "The Scoreboard Killer", is a serial killer who was convicted of murdering sixteen men but suspected of many more. He was a homosexual Air Force veteran who found many of his victims from a local military base. He had graduated from Claremont Men's College with a Bachelor's Degree in Economics, and had taken courses at Long Beach State University on teaching. His trial lasted thirteen months and was the most expensive in Orange County history.

When writing Randy I had wanted to allude that I may be questioning my sexuality or that I was gay to ensure a response. I had seen this done by others but I had a difficult time doing this, so just hinted at being different or feeling like I was treated differently, which honestly wasn't a lie, as I had long hair at the time and did feel this way. It seemed to work and we exchanged seven letters from November 2000 until December 2001. He attempted to find out what I meant, But I managed to avoid a direct answer. We talked about college basketball and he even sent me an article on my favorite coach, Mike Krzyzewski of Duke.

Cleophus Prince, "The Clairemont Killer", is a serial killer who is African American and was convicted of six murders. He came from a family where his father had murdered a man and his uncle had murdered his wife. Cleophus did a stint in the Navy before beginning his murderous way.

Cleophus was very friendly and liked to make his own greeting cards. I received two of them. One was of Scooby Doo, but the other was very interesting. It was of himself dressed as Sherlock Holmes. It was very well done.

Our correspondence went from February 2001 until July 2001 accumulating eight letters.

Bryan Maurice Jones, "The Dumpster Killer", is a serial killer who is African American and was convicted of murdering four prostitutes and disposing of their bodies in dumpsters.

Bryan preferred to be called "B.J." and claimed he was only writing one other person at the time, a fifty one year old female. He enjoyed reading poetry and we talked about sports. "B.J." stated he had aspirations of being heavyweight champion of the world in boxing after a 54-2-2 amateur career.

Our correspondence went from March 2001 until October 2001 accumulating eight letters.

"Asians tend to be passive aggressive: we don't get in fights, so it doesn't come out in little bits; it all comes out in one big act."

Wayne Lo

XV.

It was around this time I decided I needed some publicity to move my career to the next level, so I contacted a local newspaper and explained my ongoing research.

They quickly set up an interview for a feature story. Shortly thereafter the first article on me was published in the North Shore Sunday entitled Killer Letters.

I begin writing editorials on the death penalty, prison system, and such killers as Thomas Junta, the hockey dad who killed a fellow dad at the rink, and Richard Sharpe, the cross dressing wife murderer. Other killers I would write about were: Eugene McCollom, Michael McDermott, Timothy McVeigh, Richard Rogers, and Gary Sampson. They will be discussed later in this book. I had great sucess with them being published in local newspapers such as the: Boston Globe, Boston Herald, Lynn Item, North Shore Sunday, and the Salem News. I also made the USA Today as well as a couple magazines: American History Magazine, Boston Magazine, and the U.S. Catholic Magazine. Things were looking up for me as I started my next correspondence.

Wayne Lo is a local mass killer and school shooter who is Asian and was convicted of two murders and four attempted murders.

He was eighteen and would be the first school shooter I would write along with being the first subject I would speak on the phone with. During his trial a diagnosis of narcissistic personality was used.

We would become really close sharing many things and discussing virtually everything. Wayne was very intelligent and often wrote editorials on gun control that were published. We were similar in age and shared common interests in music and I felt honored when he shared photos of his family when they visited him in prison. At one point he even sent me his report card from an online college degree program he was enrolled in with Boston University.

Wayne followed the New York Yankees in professional baseball, the Sacramento Kings in professional basketball, the Atlanta Falcons in professional football, and the Detroit Red Wings in professional hockey. One thing I did notice about Wayne was he would get frustrated at times, but he would share details about others writing him as I would share whom I was writing.

He closely followed internet sales of murderabilia, especially anything of his. I often felt he enjoyed seeing something of his sold though he stated otherwise.

Our correspondence and friendship ended abruptly when I refused to send him pictures from a recent trip. I had no problem with sharing my picture but I didn't feel comfortable sharing my significant others. Perhaps I overreacted, and I understand his feeling slighted, but thought he would also see it from my point of view. Either way, it happened and he decided to end our friendship.

Our correspondence went from March 2001 until June 2005 accumulating sixty eight letters.

He managed to take a parting shot at me, saying I can sell all his letters now. That is something I have never done, sell any letter or art I have received.

"I knew the F.B.I. would get me sooner or later."
Richard Marquette

XVI.

Richard Marquette is a serial killer who was convicted of murdering one woman and was paroled after elven years only to be convicted of murdering two more women with extreme mutilation. His claim to fame was becoming the first person ever to be added to the F.B.I.'s Ten Most Wanted List as an eleventh spot.

He would include personal photos in his letters but they were long and rambled on. He would come across to me as a sad lonely man. The letters often seemed pathetic and it was hard to believe this man had such violent tendencies.

Our correspondence went from March 2001 until June 2006 accumulating forty five letters.

Calvin Jackson is a serial killer who is African American and was convicted of nine murders and what made them unique was the fact they all took place in the apartment building he lived in. His letters were some of the most graphic I've received. We discussed his preference for anal sex and his shame surrounding this. He hinted at that being the reason he had to rape and kill his victims. He felt he couldn't request it from any woman.

Calvin acknowledged that his mother physically abused him and that his grandmother spent time in a mental hospital as well as his mother's brother being a child molester. He also stated that all his correspondences over the years were criminal justice majors.

Our correspondence went from May 2001 until August 2001 accumulating six letters.

Dave Hilton Jr. is a former professional boxer from Canada who was convicted of molesting his two daughters. He was the first professional athlete I would write, and was the former brother-in-law of the late boxer Arturo Gatti. Arturo Gatti was at one time thought to have been murdered by his wife, but it was later ruled a suicide.

He was a super middleweight who appeared in forty five fights compiling a 41-2-2 career record with twenty six knockouts and would win the super middleweight world title in 2000.

Dave sent me a pic flexing after a workout, talked about how he lived with Cus D'Amato and Mike Tyson for awhile, and that he actually taught Mike Tyson how to drive. Our correspondence went from June 2001 until August 2001 accumulating two letters. Dave was later released from prison after serving his time and resumed boxing for a short period.

"When I was a law-abiding citizen on the street, I had no idea what was going on in the prisons. I feel compelled to...express my opinion for the sake of the many who cannot."

Dirk Greineder

XVII.

By now I had decided my next move education wise. I chose to go for my Master's Degree in Counseling Psychology. I also wrote my first article that was published, The Unlikely Case Of Albert DeSalvo. It was on my belief that Albert DeSalvo was not the "Boston Strangler". I then completed an online Criminal Profiling certificate course taught by world famous profiler Brent Turvey.

As busy as these pursuits kept me, I still managed to find time to attend the court proceedings of local serial killer Eugene McCollom, who was convicted of two murders, while continuing to build on my correspondences.

Dirk Greineder is a local killer who had been convicted of murdering his wife, something he still denies to this date. His defense was his wife's murder was similar to another murder around that time, which I thought was a plausible defense that wasn't taken seriously. We discussed how the correctional system in Massachusetts offers little to no rehabilitation. Years later I would meet him when I began working in the correctional system.

Our correspondence went from July 2001 until August 2001 accumulating two letters.

Raphel Cherry is a former professional football player who is African

American and was convicted of murdering his wife.

He was drafted out of the University of Hawaii in the 1985 NFL Draft by the Washington Redskins in the fifth round with the one hundred twenty second pick. He would play one season for them and two for the Detroit Lions, appearing in a total of forty two games.

Raphel played defensive back and recorded five interceptions in his NFL career. The Redskins also happened to be my favorite team.

We would mainly talk about our Redskins, but he did something memorable that touched me. After exchanging one letter it would be eight years before I heard back again. He wanted to thank me for reaching out to him eight years earlier in a time where he needed a friendly voice. All together we exchanged four letters, one in August 2001, and three from May 2009 until November 2009.

Ramon Salcido is a spree killer and family annihilator who is Latino and was convicted of murdering seven family members, including his wife and two daughters, as well as wounding two others in multiple locations. He would be the first spree killer I would write. His letters were honestly too religious for me. They were so over the top there was little else.

Our correspondence went from September 2001 until January 2002 accumulating three letters.

Also that fall I would teach my first class at North Shore Community College. The class was Mind Of A Killer. I had so much information to use and more kept coming.

Cynthia Ray is a female killer who along with her boyfriend were convicted of brutally murdering her parents to receive her portion of the estate. She would claim a childhood of physical and sexual abuse, along with her undiagnosed bipolar led to the murders.

Her letters were very forward and oozed with an overkill of sensuality. She is a woman use to using her womanly attributes to get what she wants, which is evident in her getting her boyfriend to help with the murders. She would cover my letters with kisses in bright red lipstick as well as put perfume on them.

Our correspondence was only two letters in May 2002, but left me with little doubt of her manipulative ways.

> "We all deserve to die, but that doesn't mean that I should have been the instrument by which they met their end."
>
> Kendall Francois

XVIII.

Charles Ng is a serial killer who is Asian and along with Leonard Lake raped, tortured, and killed anywhere from eleven to twenty five people. He was the first Asian serial killer I would write. Charles had been physically abused as a child before joining the Marines. He would be dishonorably discharged before becoming the submissive in the killing duo.

At trial, one that cost California twenty million, a record at the time, psychiatrist Stuart Grassian testified that Charles had a dependent personality disorder.

I would write Charles as a woman and would receive an origami heart with a swan on it. He would come the closest to Thomas Maimoni in his inability to establish a normal relationship with a woman. He came across as pathetic and inexperienced, whereas Tom was more the predator. In just his second letter he sent me forms to complete to visit him even though we lived on opposite sides of the country.

He mentioned his only other correspondences being from women in Europe. Our correspondence went from June 2002 until September 2002 accumulating three letters. Leonard Lake would commit suicide upon capture in 1985.

Kendall Francois was a serial killer who was African American and convicted of murdering eight women. He was an Army veteran who was HIV positive, and the second subject I would speak on the phone with.

Kendall would draw me a Christmas card with what looked like the Mr. Men characters on it. He followed the New York Yankees in professional baseball and the New York Rangers in professional hockey. He was another of the killers that seemed so laid back and incapable of such horrific violence.

The fact he kept the bodies in the house, and not buried in the basement would be a red flag for mental illness such as Harrison Graham's case. But no diagnosis was brought up that I found which leads me to believe he kept the bodies to re-visit sexually but also for company as he was so socially awkward. That would be similar to serial killer Jeffrey Dahmer.

Our correspondence went from 2002 until 2003 accumulating twenty four letters. Kendall died in prison on September 11th in 2014 at the age of forty three.

Thomas Dillon was a serial killer who was convicted of five murders of hunters he hunted for sport. I wrote to him as a woman and he would tell me that he was only writing two other people at that time, both men, one in Michigan and the other in Ohio.

He told me that before his arrest he visited Boston and explored The Freedom Trail. He expressed his love for true crime novels and dislike of country music. He also told me of being charged by the prison of threatening an African American correctional officer.

Our correspondence went from August 2002 until April 2003 accumulating nine letters. Tom died in prison on October 21st in 2011 at the age of sixty one.

"Killing prostitutes had become an obsession with me. I could not stop myself. It was like a drug."

Peter Sutcliffe

XIX.

Peter Sutcliffe, "The Yorkshire Ripper", is a serial killer from England who was convicted of murdering thirteen women. During his trial a diagnosis of paranoid schizophrenia was used.

I would first write to him as myself to which I received a letter from his prison psychiatrist stating he didn't wish to correspond. I then decided to write back sometime later as a woman and it paid off. I received a letter, but at first was skeptical as it was signed by Peter Coonan. I didn't initially believe it was him until I researched and found out he changed his name to honor his Irish heritage, taking his great grandfather's name, Coonan.

Since being in prison Coonan has been attacked numerous times by many different inmates, sustaining multiple injuries including the loss of an eye. He said he smiled when he read I followed the British science fiction show Doctor Who and asked if there was a Titanic Museum in Springfield. He stated his favorite television show was Heartbeat, which was remade over here in the states, but cancelled after only one season.

He also mentioned a girl from the states recently writing him, but she talked about Hitler and Satanism so he had his psychiatrist write her back saying he wasn't interested in corresponding, much like he had done to me initially.

Our correspondence went from September 2002 until November 2002 accumulating four letters.

Douglas Clark, one half of the "Sunset Strip Killers", is a serial killer who along with his partner Carol Bundy were convicted of murdering six people. He was an Air Force veteran whose family was always moving, making it hard to form friendships. He would engage in necrophilia with his victims and his letters reminded me of those from Lawrence Bittaker. Same attitude and grievances.

He would show frustration at my questions, stating he was tired of being asked the same questions over and over. Any chance he got he would blame his accomplice Carol Bundy and explained all the legal evidence to back it up.

Our correspondence went from October 2002 until December 2002 accumulating three letters. Carol Bundy died in prison on December 9th in 2003 at the age of sixty one from heart failure.

Keith Jesperson, "The Happy Face Killer", is a serial killer who was suspected of at least eight murders, with claims of many more. As a child he was physically and sexually abused as well as having a history of torturing animals. As an adult he grew to an imposing six feet seven inches. He had two failed suicide attempts around the time of his arrest.

His letters were highlighted by his short temper and mood swings. He got irritated at me when I stated I would get into something next letter, as if I had been continually avoiding it, when in fact we only exchanged two letters.

He mentioned having completed thirty six drawings in 2002, but also about having an upcoming hearing at the prison over his art and its sales.

Our correspondence went from November 2002 until January 2003.

In an interesting twist to the story, his daughter Melissa Moore published a book, Shattered Silence: The Untold Story of a Serial Killer's Daughter, in 2009. Then in 2015 she hosted a television series Monster In My Family on the Lifetime Movies Network that has now completed two seasons. In the show she facilitates meetings between relatives of serial killers and family members of their victims.

"I sit here all alone. I am always alone. I don't know who I am. I want to be something I can never be. I try so hard every day. But in the end, I hate myself for what I've become."

Kip Kinkel

XX.

Kip Kinkel is a spree killer and a school shooter who was convicted of first murdering his parents at home before going to his school the next day and killing two students and wounding twenty five others.

Fifteen at the time of his crimes, Kip had already been diagnosed with dyslexia and had been seeing a psychologist for depression. At his trial paranoid schizophrenia would be brought up as a possible cause of his crimes.

We would only exchange one letter and it was very brief in December 2002. He was twenty at that time but seemed so shy and to suffer from low self-esteem in my opinion. He even responded to my request to correspond with doubt saying, "you may not like me".

Tina Marie Cornelius is a female killer who was convicted of killing her own children. This is often referred to as filicide.

I had written to men who had killed their children, parents, wives, and other family members before in mass and spree events, and to Cynthia Ray who killed her parents, but there is something about a woman killing a child she gave birth to that sets it above the other cases.

Tina Cornelius worked as a topless dancer at the time of her crimes. Her crimes stand out a bit more than her contemporaries, Andrea Yates and Susan Smith because of the brutality. She first suffocated the daughter then bashed in the boy's skull with a rock before tossing their bodies off a cliff.

We talked about music. She acknowledged Moody Blues was the only concert she had ever been to. She loved the band Boston, as well as Metallica and a new song by Evanescence. She completed a college course in Biology during our correspondence earning a B.

I would send her brochures on Salem which she enjoyed reading. She would send me a beautifully decorated envelope with flowers drawn on it and 'thank you'. She also drew a butterfly on one of her letters to me and expressed a love of fast cars and big trucks.

Our correspondence went from February 2003 until June 2003 accumulating six letters.

In March of 2003 I would teach my second class at North Shore Community College. This class was Serial Killers Of Literature And Film. The North Shore Sunday would write an article on it entitled Class Of Death. With opportunities before me, I continued writing.

Richard Farley is a mass killer convicted of murdering seven people and injuring four others at ESL Inc. as a result of his anger after being repeatedly rejected by Laura Black.

Richard was a Navy veteran whose persistent stalking of Laura led to the first anti-stalking laws nationwide. Brooke Shields would later portray her in a film adaption of the case entitled, I Can Make You Love Me.

My initial letter would take four months before getting a response. He claimed it got lost amongst his legal paperwork. Richard didn't waste time before updating me on Laura's status, claiming he had heard she was working on her doctorate and had made two hundred fifty thousand as a consultant for the I Can Make You Love Me movie.

He would also express his views on women, stating they would take over television in the upcoming years. He professed a love of science fiction and following the San Francisco 49ers in professional football.

Our correspondence went from October 2003 until December 2003 accumulating two letters.

Also around this time I would start presenting a lecture to local colleges and libraries. The lecture was entitled Imprisoned Artists: The Art Of Famous Murderers.

"Every life has meaning."
Robert Lee Yates

XXI.

Hadden Clark is a serial killer who was convicted of two murders but suspected of many more. He was also the answer to a question I was asked frequently. Who has creeped me out the most from those I have communicated with? My answer has always been Hadden Clark.

He was a Navy veteran who suffered from paranoid schizophrenia and whose brother Bradfield had strangled a woman and whose alcoholic father had committed suicide. Hadden was also bullied and tortured animals.

Hadden cannibalized his victims and immortalized them in his art. He constantly drew little girls on all his envelopes and letters. They would be giving sign language and looked like the same girl with just different color hair.

He asked multiple times if I would send him Girl Scout or Playboy calendars, to which I always ignored. I had been asked to get Playboys before, but Girl Scouts was a first.

The most bizarre request however was that he said he would be willing to share details of his crimes if I was willing to write him as "Michelle". Michelle just happened to be the name of one of his victims.

A few years before I had started writing him he agreed to personally lead police to graves of some victims on the condition they got him women's clothing to wear while out on the search. Authorities agreed but no graves were ever found, but authorities did unearth a bucket with over two hundred pieces of women's jewelry. Trophies perhaps from unaccounted victims of this strange man.

Our correspondence went from January 2004 until January 2006 accumulating eleven letters and numerous drawings.

Henry Louis Wallace is a serial killer who is African American and was convicted of the murders of nine women. He was a Navy veteran who abused crack cocaine.

He had neat writing but was very suspicious of my motives for writing him as he had been taking advantage of by murderabilia dealers in the past.

He claimed much of what the website Crime Library published about him was "straight bullshit". He also talked about struggling to adjust to prison life and about writing a "troubled" boy in Omaha.

As with many of the other subjects we discussed sports and I learned that he followed the San Antonio Spurs in professional basketball, the Duke Blue Devils in college basketball, and the Carolina Panthers in professional football.

Our correspondence went from January 2004 until November 2004 accumulating six letters.

Also around January 2004 I would have my collection of inmate art displayed at the Melrose Public Library. It would create a bit of controversy, but also garner great reviews. In February of 2004 the Lawrence Eagle Tribune would publish an article on me entitled Corresponding With Serial Killers. Each article kept encouraging me to write.

Robert Lee Yates is a serial killer who was convicted of fifteen murders. He was an Army veteran who earned two Armed Forces Expeditionary Medals, three Army Achievement Medals, three Army Commendation Medals, and three Meritorious Service Medals. He also engaged in necrophilia with his victims.

His letters were of the overzealous variety concerning religion. We really didn't talk about much and thus it was a short correspondence. This would be my choice. I always found this disappointing and felt Robert could have a lot to say should he choose to.

Our correspondence went from April 2004 until October 2004 accumulating four letters.

"I made my own grave by being sloppy."

Robert Pickton

XXII.

Ralph Andrews was a serial killer who was convicted of one murder but suspected of many more. He made confessions of numerous ones to a fellow inmate who was working with authorities and recording their conversations.

His writing was sloppy and appeared rushed. He had previously been married but stated he wasn't "a one woman man". He expressed a love for outdoor activities such as camping, cross country & downhill skiing, fishing, and hunting.

Our correspondence was in May 2004 accumulating one letter. Ralph died in prison on January 31st in 2006 at the age of sixty.

Robert Pickton is a serial killer from Canada who was suspected in the deaths, and possible cannibalization of at least twenty six women. He had a low IQ of eighty six, but had very neat writing.

In his letters he talked about the guards putting him in a cell with feces on the floor, a clogged toilet, and a bed frame but no mattress. He would also accuse the guards of poisoning his food.

He did however state he was enrolled in a class on agriculture. Ironic since he owned a pig farm where he was torturing, killing, and disposing of his victims. Many of which were fed to the pigs and some even sold to the public mixed in with the pork.

Our correspondence went from May 2004 until January 2005 accumulating two letters.

Carolyn Warmus, "The Fatal Attraction Murderess" was a female killer who was convicted of murdering her lover's wife after a period of harassment and stalking. Her parents divorced when she was eight.

Carolyn's story was portrayed in the cult classic movie Fatal Attraction staring Glenn Close and Michael Douglas.

Carolyn was a University of Michigan graduate with a Bachelor's Degree in Psychology followed by a Master's Degree in Elementary Education from Columbia. After completing college she began to work with her victim and her husband.

They would have a torrid affair before he would break it off and jump start Carolyn's anger.

Shortly before I would write her she sued the Department of Corrections for sexual abuse by the guards and won a ten thousand dollar lawsuit. Warmus had somehow managed to provide officials with an officer's semen.

Her first letter to me was a form letter requesting money for her legal fees. I found this to be revealing. I would write back stating I don't give money to someone who can't even take the time to answer me with a personal letter.

She would quickly send one, but only to personally request the money. I would not give her any.

One thing I have learned is the women I have written tend to ask for money more than the men.

Our correspondence went from June 2004 until July 2004 accumulating two letters.

Carolyn would be released from prison on June 17th in 2019 after serving twenty seven years.

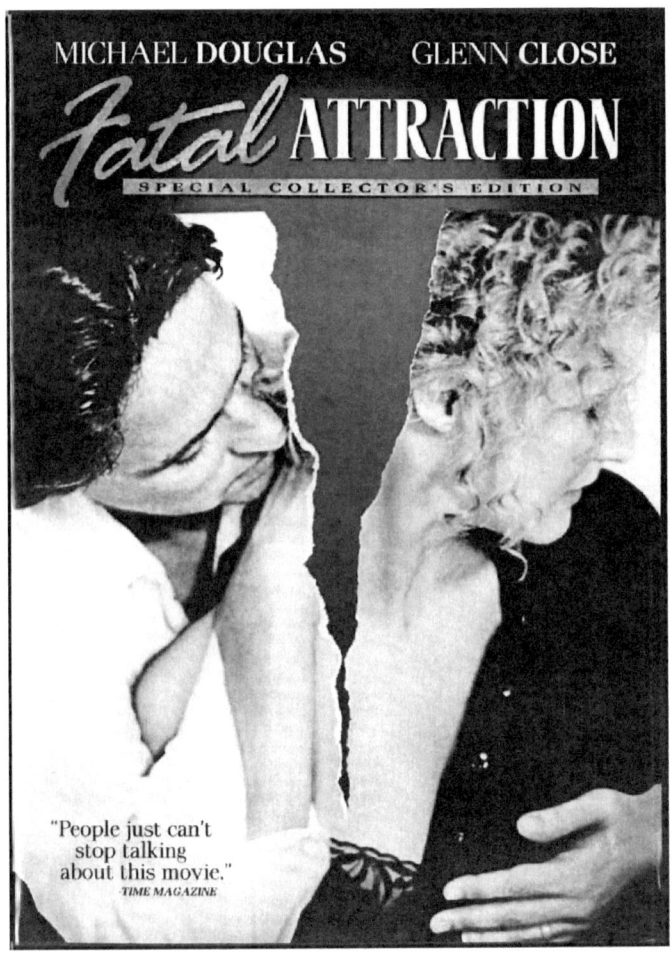

Paramount Pictures 1987

> "I'm waiting for the woman to die."
>
> Orville Lynn Majors response to a hospital employee when found alone in the hospital's ICU and asked what he was doing.

XXIII.

Nathaniel Bar-Jonah was a serial killer suspected in the disappearances of numerous children, the vast majority of which were young boys. He was a homosexual cannibal.

His first assault on a child was when he was just seven years old. The victim was five. Nathan was a large man who cast a frightening presence, one can only imagine the fear he instilled in these children.

His letters to me were always on stationary that contained recipes on it such as: Honeydew Kiwi Fruit Smoothie, Jalapeno Stuffed Pork Tenderloin, Jamaican Chicken Salad, Shrimp Stuffing, and White Chocolate Cheesecake.

He claimed he has had almost one hundred and fifty pen pals in seven countries since he had been incarcerated. Those countries included: Canada, England, France, Holland, Poland, Sweden, and the United States.

He talked about trying to publish a book of his poetry and his plans to open his own restaurant upon release from prison. He claimed innocence to the charges and had plans for his restaurant already drawn up. Furthermore he was studying psychology through an online program by University of Israel.

However, what scared me the most was his claims to have visited my precious city of Salem, Massachusetts, touring the famed House Of Seven Gables, not too far from my home.

Our correspondence went from January 2005 until January 2006 accumulating five letters. Nathan died in prison on April 13th in 2008 at the age of fifty one from a heart attack.

Ward Weaver Jr. is a serial killer who was convicted of two murders but suspected of many more. He also may be the strongest link for a genetic predisposition I have come across. This link starts with him and continues for two generations.

His son Ward Weaver III, a Naval Reservist veteran and heavy drinker, was responsible for the murders of two young girls while the grandson Francis Weaver was convicted of murdering a drug dealer.

Ward Weaver Jr.'s writing was very small and difficult to read. Luckily for me he started to type his responses after the second one.

He would ask me if I knew of Shelburne Falls, Massachusetts, as he had friends there. He also talked about a friend on death row for the past twenty five years that was set to be executed.

Surprisingly he didn't follow sports like the vast majority of the others did. I did find it funny that he said this on stationary that had pictures of baseballs, basketballs, footballs, and hockey pucks/sticks.

Our correspondence went from January 2005 until December 2005 accumulating four letters.

Beginning in February 2005 I would create and run a True Crime Book Group at the Chelmsford Public Library. With a little luck maybe this novel will someday be discussed at one. Also around this time author Katherine Ramsland mentioned me in an article she wrote for Crime Library. This was a famous website owned by Court TV and later TruTV that had articles on most every famous mass, serial, and spree killer. In her article she mentioned information she obtained from the Lawrence Eagle Tribune article on me, Corresponding With Serial Killers. The success of this group and being mentioned like that encouraged me to keep writing.

Orville Lynn Majors was a serial killer and an angel of death who was suspected of the murders of as many as one hundred thirty patients. He was a homosexual and told me he preferred to be called "Lynn" and asked me to send him a picture of myself and he would send one of himself in return.

Our correspondence was in March 2005 accumulating one letter. Lynn died in prison on September 24th in 2017 at the age of fifty six from heart failure.

"In the end, it all comes to choices to turn stumbling blocks into stepping stones."
Scott Peterson

XXV.

Around this time, June of 2005 I achieved my Master's Degree in Counseling Psychology from Anna Maria College. I put a lot of time and effort into achieving this milestone, but I wasn't alone in the pursuit. My parents equally worked hard over the years to help with support and tuitions.

The ink on my diploma was still drying when the next correspondence would arrive.

Scott Peterson is a family annihilator who was convicted of murdering his wife and their unborn child. He denied the crime then and still denies it today. His conviction would cost the state of California two million six hundred forty thousand dollars.

He was a media sensation and women would write him by the hundreds. As a result I would write him as a woman. This would be the final time I would use this strategy to garner a response.

Due to the vast amount of people, mainly women, that wrote him, I would get a form letter from the family.

On one of these letters was the recipe for Lavender Cookies, a favorite of Laci. There was also an offer to subscribe to a newsletter for fifteen dollars a year. This would come out every four to six weeks.

Our correspondence went from June 2005 until July 2005 accumulating two letters.

Anthony Joyner is a serial killer who is African American and was convicted of the murders of six women at the rest home he worked at. He was unique in the fact that he found all his victims at his work, killed them at his work, and left them at his work. In this way he was similar to Calvin Jackson who found all his victims at his apartment complex, killed them there, and left them there.

Of all my serial killer subjects they are the only two to fit this pattern. The angel of death serial killers come closest but their murders were less violent and concealed.

His letters were religious, but not over the top like some of the others. He did proclaim his innocence and the fact he had written nearly three hundred letters asking for help since his incarceration.

He was proud of the fact that he had recently graduated a culinary program at the prison, and that his family were all respectable members of society without any arrest histories.

Our correspondence went from August 2005 until December 2005 accumulating two letters.

In October 2005 the Northern Essex Community College Observer would publish an article on me entitled Lecturer Exposes The Psyche Of The Serial Killer. Again I was encouraged to write to more killers.

Alfred Gaynor is a local serial killer who is African American and was convicted of the murders of nine women. During the time the murders were ongoing I actually did my own profile of the subject that I shared with family and friends which ended up being spot on when he was identified.

I wrote him using the interest in art approach after seeing his art and it's controversial selling of it making the newspapers. The art itself was not the best, it reminded me of Richard Ramirez's, very basic and juvenile subject matter. Maybe one out of every ten pieces of his showed promise.

With that in mind, I was shocked when he asked for two hundred and fifty dollars for a drawing. Obviously I never purchased it.

Beside that his spelling was horrible as he made numerous grammatical errors throughout the letter. I would never receive another letter after turning down his deal.

However, less than two years later I would meet him while working in the prison system.

Our correspondence was in November 2005 accumulating one letter.

"People do things when you are watching they wouldn't do if you were there."
Dennis Rabbitt

XXV.

Gerald Parker, "The Bedroom Basher", is a serial killer who is African American and was convicted of six murders. His first prison term was a six year stint for the rape of a fourteen year old girl committed while a Marine.

He would acknowledge his guilt and remorse to me, and that Court TV airs a show on his case every ninety days in California. His favorite authors were John LeCarre and Robert Ludlum. He also followed politics intently.

Our correspondence was in December 2005 accumulating one letter.

Ramsey Dardar is a former professional football player who is African American and was convicted of numerous burglary and possession of stolen goods charges. During his legal proceedings his lawyer stated his IQ was seventy one.

He was drafted out of LSU in the 1983 NFL Draft by the St. Louis Cardinals in the third round with the seventy first pick. He would play one season for them, appearing in sixteen games.

Ramsey played offensive line but injuries limited his career to that one season.

He was very gracious to me in his letters even offering to make me a matching belt and wallet in the leather shop at the prison. I was asked to choose between alligator, lizard, ostrich, or snake skins for the material.

I was informed that ESPN Magazine and Sports Illustrated had recently visited him at the prison for information on a piece they were working on. He also expressed regret for not getting his degree while at LSU.

In what was a surprise to me, he informed me he played contact football at the prison, and actually sent me a picture of him being presented a trophy for being named MVP.

Our correspondence went from April 2006 until May 2006 accumulating two letters.

Dennis Rabbitt, "The South Side Rapist", is a serial rapist who was convicted of twenty nine rapes but suspected in as many as one hundred.

Early on in his life his mother was murdered at the hands of his step father. Dennis himself was stabbed in prison by three inmates in 2005 which resulted in him being placed into protective custody.

His writing was very neat and he acknowledged being a big sports fan. During his time in prison he stated he had repented his sins. He also mentioned he doesn't get much mail.

Our correspondence went from May 2006 until December 2006 accumulating four letters.

"They should have killed me before when they sentenced me. Punishment wasn't prison time, but death."

Todd Rizzo

XXVI.

Todd Rizzo was convicted of murdering a thirteen year old boy. At the time of the murder, Todd himself was only eighteen and an ex Marine. He was obsessed with serial killers, especially Jeffrey Dahmer. He was said to collect serial killer trading cards to.

Todd may have had the most perfect writing of anyone I corresponded with. He also put "3,185th day of incarceration" under the date on the letter.

He made it a point for me to know he was no longer obsessed with serial killers. I made the admission to him that I had written Michael Ross, whom he shared time with on death row. It seemed he would compare a lot about himself to Michael. His biggest point was to let me know he wasn't religious like Michael was.

Todd basically told me he would write me because he currently wrote two males and four females so another male would "almost even things up".

Our correspondence was in June 2006 accumulating one letter.

Monte Ralph Rissell is a serial killer who was convicted of five murders. His IQ was one hundred twenty, and his father left the family when he was only seven.

His reason for answering my initial letter was "it was a bad tv night". He was also concerned I may be a "weirdo" as he felt most who wrote him were.

He claimed most of the females who wrote him talked sex or marriage and the guys usually talked about Satanism. He figured with me being from Salem, I would be the later.

Monte acknowledged that his older brother and sister don't speak to him and that retired F.B.I. profiler Robert Ressler writes him as well as visits three to four times a year. I was personally impressed that Robert Ressler would do that and have always respected him.

We would find common ground in sports as Monte was a diehard Washington Redskins fan like me. He claimed to have seen them play in person many times including at Super Bowl VII vs the Miami Dolphins. He was so dedicated a fan that he even got into a fight with another inmate when that inmate tried to put on the Dallas Cowboys vs Philadelphia Eagles game before the Washington Redskins vs New York Giants game had ended.

Monte was also a New York Yankees fan in professional baseball, a Duke Blue Devils and Kansas Jayhawks fan in college basketball, a Notre Dame Fighting Irish, University of Southern California Trojans, and Virginia Cavaliers fan in college football.

But when it came to professional basketball he seemed to follow stars or winners, as he was first a Julius Erving and Philadelphia 76ers fan, then he became a Michael Jordan and Chicago Bulls fan, and currently was a San Antonio Spurs fan.

Our correspondence went from July 2006 until December 2006 accumulating five letters.

Darion Conner is a former professional football player who is African

American and was convicted of DUI manslaughter and vehicular homicide.

He was drafted out of Jackson State in the 1990 NFL Draft by the Atlanta Falcons in the second round with the twenty eighth pick. He would play four seasons for them, then play one for the New Orleans Saints, one for the Carolina Panthers, and two for the Philadelphia Eagles, appearing in one hundred fourteen games.

Darion played linebacker and recorded thirty three sacks and one interception in his NFL career.

Darion resurfaced in the Arena League with the Tampa Bay Storm. He would play seven seasons for them, appearing in fifty eight games while recording eleven sacks in his AFL career.

His letters were very religious but he was gracious for me writing him. He talked about the "bad mistakes" he has made in his life and his two daughters Desiree and Destiny. He would sign his letters Darion AF #56.

Our correspondence went from September 2006 until April 2007 accumulating four letters.

"No matter what I get hit with, I keep on coming. The only way to stop me is to kill me."

Clifford Etienne

XXVII.

Carl Drew is a local killer who was convicted of one murder. He was the leader of a satanic cult who were suspected and tied to other murders.

I asked him about the book Mortal Remains by Henry Scammell, to which he responded, "the book is all lies". He would then ask my opinion on his art which I mentioned in my letter and he recommended I check out his webpage on prisonerlife.com to learn more about him.

Our correspondence was in February 2007 accumulating one letter.

Clifford Etienne, "The Black Rhino", is a former professional boxer who is African American and was convicted of armed robbery, attempted murder of a police officer, and kidnapping. His lawyers would argue brain injury from boxing and drug use as the uncontrollable factors that led him to commit these acts.

Clifford learned how to box while in prison compiling a 30-0 record there before a parole gave him a chance to fight professionally.

He was a heavyweight who appeared in thirty five fights compiling a 29-4-2 career record with twenty knockouts which would include a loss to former undisputed heavyweight champion "Iron" Mike Tyson.

Prior to writing him and his incarceration I actually saw him box in person at the Mohegan Sun Casino in Uncasville, Connecticut on April 27th 2002. He won that fight vs Terrence Lewis by unanimous decision.

He didn't take long to let me know that his trial attorney "took his money and ran". He would sign his letter with Clifford "The Black Rhino" Etienne.

Our correspondence was in February 2007 accumulating one letter.

Before I would receive a new correspondence I would begin working in the state's supermax facility, the Souza-Baranowski Correctional Center. The facility was named after a correctional officer, James Souza, and an instructor, Alfred Baranowski, who were both killed in 1972 during an escape attempt from MCI-Norfolk.

The prison has nearly four hundred cameras and has been the home of some of Massachusett's worst killers as well as the scene of many a murder and suicide. The facility made national headlines when on August 23rd 2003 a convicted murderer, Joseph Druce, strangled convicted pedophile priest John Geoghan, and again on April 19th 2017 when former New England Patriot Aaron Hernandez hung himself.

My position was a General Population Counselor and occasionally I would be sent to MCI-Cedar Junction, or more commonly known as Walpole, which at the time was still a maximum security facility. It has since been downgraded to medium.

Among the many murderers I would see and or interact with there and at Walpole were: Michael Bizanowicz, Joseph Druce, Jamie Fuller, Alfred Gaynor, Dirk Greineder, Paul Leahy, Christopher McCowen, Michael McDermott, George Nassar, and Daniel Tavares, as well as serial rapists Wilfred Evicci and Che Sosa.

Michael Bizanowicz was convicted of murdering a mother and her daughter.

Jamie Fuller was convicted of murdering his fourteen year old girlfriend. At the time of his crime he was sixteen and abusing steroids. Paul Leahy was convicted of murdering a woman in the bathroom of a Burger King at a rest stop in the middle of the night. Christopher McCowen is African American and was convicted of murdering Christa Worthington on Cape Cod. It was a case that generated national attention. Michael McDermott is a mass killer and a Navy veteran who was convicted of murdering seven people at Edgewater Technology in Wakefield. Schizophrenia was used as a diagnosis during his trial.

George Nassar, who was convicted of one murder at sixteen and was paroled after thirteen years only to be convicted of a second murder is often regarded as the real "Boston Strangler" by many experts, a belief I agree with. He has been diagnosed with schizophrenic tendencies but also with an IQ of one hundred seventy two. Wilfred Evicci was convicted of two rapes and suspected in others and Che Sosa who is African American was convicted of two rapes and suspected in others. He is the most feared inmate in the Massachusetts prison system. Over the years he has attacked numerous staff and even his own lawyer. He also convinced a nurse to help him in an escape attempt which thankfully didn't work. I will never forget the way he looked at me, it sent chills down my back.

Daniel Tavares is a serial killer who was convicted of murdering his mother and was paroled after sixteen years only to be convicted of three more murders and at one time was suspected of being "The New Bedford Highway Killer", who was responsible for at least nine murders.

The remaining men, Joseph Druce, Alfred Gaynor, and Dirk Greineder, I have already discussed. Unfortunately I will not get into the specifics of any conversations I may have had with any of these men as they would have been work related.

Richard Crafts, "The Wood Chipper Murderer", was convicted of murdering his wife in Connecticut's first murder conviction without a body. The body was believed to have been disposed of in a wood chipper.

He would type his correspondence and the majority of the content was asking me if I had access to a law library, if so where, and could he call from time to time for help.

Our correspondence was in August 2007 accumulating one letter.

"This is the Zodiac. The Zodiac will kill twelve signs in the belt. When the Zodiacal light is seen Zodiac will spread fear."

Heriberto Seda

XXVIII.

Phillip Jablonski is a serial killer who was convicted of murdering one woman and was paroled after twelve years only to be convicted of four more murders of women. He was an Army veteran with a long history of violent and sexual assaults who married Carol Spadoni while in prison for the first murder after she answered an ad he placed.

He would admit to me he was bisexual and proud. He would also acknowledge being molested by a man when he was only five. But worst, he would brag about raping and pimping out cellmates over the years, and having no regrets or remorse about anything he has done.

The one highlight was his art. Phillip was another subject who did his drawings right on the envelope. He also appeared to be loyal to his pen pals as he claimed to have been writing some people sixteen years now.

Our correspondence was in August 2007 accumulating one letter.

Gary Sampson is a local spree killer convicted of three murders. He had been physically abused as a child and diagnosed with an antisocial personality disorder.

He followed the Boston Red Sox in professional baseball and the New England Patriots in professional football but he preferred camping, fishing, and hiking to sports.

Gary would send me a picture and claim that a woman has all his files but not written a single page of a proposed book. Unfortunately he felt his lawyers would advise against writing me so he ended our friendship.

Our correspondence went from December 2007 until July 2008 accumulating four letters.

Heriberto Seda, "The Zodiac Killer", is a serial killer who is Latino and was convicted of three murders and six attempted murders. He was an East Coast modern day copycat of the original West Coast San Francisco killer.

His correspondence was alarming to me as his main goal from me was to obtain information such as bullet energy, velocity, and weight for the following rifle cartridges: 600 Nitro Express, 6mm PPC, and the .405 Winchester. He also requested no copies from the computer just information as pictures would have been confiscated.

It is clear by this request he is still fantasizing of committing more murders. Obviously I didn't give him any of the information he wanted. As a result of this he didn't answer me again.

Our correspondence was in December 2007 accumulating one letter.

While in prison Eddie, as he liked to be called, has been involved with Synthia-Blast, a pre-op transsexual Latin King member also in prison for murder. Synthia has acknowledged having sex with some of New York's most famous murderers and also of being Eddie's first kiss. Eddie was thirty five at the time.

"To think about the stuff that I did, I try not to. I would have nightmares."
Wesley Shermantine

XXIX.

Jack Trawick was a serial killer convicted of two murders but suspected of many more.

He would tell me that seventy five to eighty percent of those who have written him are females between the ages of eighteen to thirty. Those requesting sexual violence were ten times those who were not. Of those requesting the violence seventy five percent were female.

When I informed Jack that some of his letters were being sold online he stated that he knew about it and claimed some of them were fakes. He warned me the content of his letters would be limited after someone set up a website and pretended to be him.

During the time we corresponded the 2008 Summer Olympics were happening in Beijing and Jack would let me know who he was following: "Go female swim team, go female volleyball team."

Our correspondence went from August 2008 until October 2008 accumulating two letters. Jack was executed at the Holmon Correctional Facility on June 11th in 2009 at the age of sixty two by lethal injection.

His last meal consisted of fried chicken, french fries, onion soup and a roll. His last words were: "I wish to apologize to the people whom I have hurt and I ask for their forgiveness. I don't deserve it but I do ask for it."

Larry Bright is a serial killer who was convicted of murdering eight women. He had a long history of abusing alcohol, cocaine, marijuana, and painkillers.

He would make it clear from the start that he did not wish to discuss his case. He did however tell me of his fondness for reading western novels.

Our correspondence was sometime in 2009 accumulating one letter.

Wesley Shermantine, one of "The Speed Freak Killers", is a serial killer who was convicted of four murders, three along with his partner Loren Herzog. They were suspected of as many as seventy two murders and earned their nickname due to their methamphetamine use. Wesley had also been physically abused by his alcoholic mother as a child.

By most accounts Wesley was the more dominant of the two. In prison however, he was very calm and laid back. He was enrolled in a prison hobby program where he studied Bob Ross, the late host of The Joy Of Painting. Growing up I happened to be a fan of his show.

Due to his new hobby he would ask me to send any donations towards painting supplies to his attorneys whose contact information he could provide me.

Our correspondence was in February 2010 accumulating one letter.

Later that year in September Loren Herzog would be paroled only to commit suicide in January 2012 when Wesley disclosed the locations of more bodies which would implicate Loren and send him back to prison. This seems to further establish Wesley's dominance over Loren.

Much controversy arose from Wesley's participation due to the fact he was being paid for the information.

"I look back now on what I did and agree with you now that it was heinous, that I was heinous."

Genene Jones

XXX.

These next few chapters and killers feature individuals whose letters did not have dates on them. At the time I was not as OCD as I am now and didn't keep track. So these correspondences will fit in anywhere after the first five or six killers I wrote and before the last killer in the previous chapter.

Natasha Cornett is a female mass killer who was convicted along with fellow cult members Jason Bryant, Karen Howell, Edward Mullins, Joseph Risner, and Crystal Sturgill of three murders in the family annihilation of the Lillelid family. The father, mother, and one of the two sons were killed, luckily the second and youngest son survived.

Natasha was said to have been diagnosed bipolar before joining the group that was immersed in drugs and the goth culture. They would soon leave Pikeville, Kentucky and head to New Orleans encountering the Lillelid family on the way.

Natasha loved the fact that I lived in Salem yet also stated that she is so different than the media portrays her. If I was looking for that I would be disappointed.

Our correspondence accumulated one letter.

As I mentioned in a previous chapter Natasha and Christa Pike would attempt to kill a fellow inmate in 2001.

Darryl Henley is a former professional football player who is African American and was convicted of trafficking cocaine and attempted murder of a federal judge and a witness.

He was drafted out of UCLA in the 1989 NFL Draft by the Los Angeles Rams in the second round with the fifty third pick. He would play six seasons for them appearing in seventy six games.

Darryl played defensive back and recorded twelve interceptions in his NFL career.

Our first topic of discussion was the book Pros And Cons: The Criminals Who Play In The NFL by Jeff Benedict and Don Yaeger. I had remembered Darryl as a player but had been unaware of his legal issues until I read this book which details the circumstances.

Darryl would praise his family calling his parents "awesome". He had equally good things to say about his brothers, proud to say that older brother Thomas was a Stanford graduate and younger brother Eric was a Rice graduate.

I would tell him I was a Washington Redskins fan and he told me about playing at Foxboro against the New England Patriots his rookie year. But my favorite conversation was when he asked my opinion on former NFL linebacker Ray Lewis. I was not a fan of Ray Lewis and will go to my grave believing he got away with two murders. The book Pros And Cons also highlighted his case.

Our correspondence accumulated four letters.

Genene Jones is a female serial killer and an angel of death who was convicted of two murders of children but suspected of up to sixty murders.

Her letters were very religious and she made offers to pray for anyone in my family. There was no mention of her crimes what so ever.

Our correspondence accumulated three letters.

It should be noted that Genene was scheduled for release from the Texas prison system some time in 2018 due to prison overcrowding.

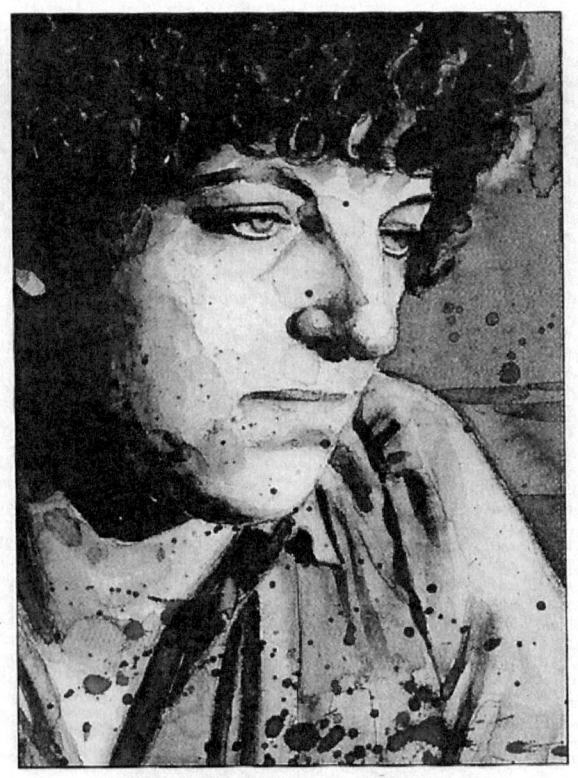

GENENE JONES

> "I would only hope that the Community Release Board will never see fit to parole Mr. Kearney because he appears to be an insult to humanity."
>
> Superior Court Judge Paul Breckenridge Jr.'s opinion on Patrick Kearney

XXXI.

Patrick Kearney, "The Trash Bag Killer", is a serial killer who was convicted of twenty one murders after admitting to as many as forty three. He was a homosexual necrophiliac who had been bullied as a child.

Patrick asked me if I could scan and send his math formulas to people via email. I would send him the Schrodinger equation for which he was very grateful.

The most interesting thing he would do was to randomly change colors of his pen from black to blue, red, or green. Being the mathematical genius he was I assumed he was trying to use some type of code but nothing appeared to make sense.

Patrick didn't follow sports but was interested if I wrote any inmates from foreign countries because he could write French and Spanish and would help me.

Our correspondence accumulated three letters.

Bobby Joe Maxwell, "The Skid Row Stabber", was a serial killer who is African American and was convicted of two murders and suspected of ten or eleven total. At one point those two murder convictions were overturned but to little avail as he was retried on them and indicted on an additional three.

His crimes had a satanic element to them which was ironic since his writing was over religious and he claimed his innocence. He also informed me he wasn't initially going to write me and had to pray on it first.

Our correspondence accumulated one letter. Bobby died in prison in 2019.

Art Schlichter is a former professional football player who was convicted of numerous fraud charges. He has one of the most intense gambling addictions I've ever seen. At one of his more recent trials it was stated doctors believe he has chronic traumatic encephalopathy due to numerous concussions during his playing days. He is also battling Parkinson's Disease and dementia now as well.

He was drafted out of Ohio State University in the 1982 NFL Draft by the Baltimore Colts in the first round with the fourth pick, a few picks ahead of Hall Of Fame running back Marcus Allen. He would play three seasons for them appearing in thirteen games.

Art played quarterback and recorded one thousand six yards passing and three touchdowns passing in his NFL career. Due to his gambling he was suspended numerous times and finally banished from the NFL.

Art resurfaced in the Canadian Football League with the Ottawa Rough Riders playing one season with them while recording six hundred fifty eight yards passing and three touchdowns passing in his CFL career.

From there Art went to the Arena Football League playing first for the Detroit Drive for two seasons then the Cincinnati Rockers for one season. He would record six thousand sixty seven yards passing and one hundred five touchdowns passing in his AFL career earning league MVP in 1990.

He would talk about his playing days with me and how he played against Hall Of Famers John Elway, Dan Marino, and Walter Payton. When I told him I was a Washington Redskins fan he told me he played them twice in his brief career. He remembered playing in Foxboro against the New England Patriots. He also remembered playing against ex New England Patriot Tony Collins in the Arena League. Tony suffered through a long drug addiction and Art seemed to feel a connection with him.

When I told him of the trading card of his I owned, he would tell me he sold all his memorabilia to pay for legal fees. Art also gave me his mother's address and phone number in case I ever lost touch and to set up times to call him. I believe I did speak with her once but Art and I never did get to speak on the phone.

Our correspondence accumulated three letters.

> "I don't know what love is. Two words I don't like to use is 'love' and 'sorry', because I'm about hate."
>
> Tommy Lynn Sells

XXXII.

Tommy Lynn Sells was a serial killer who was convicted of one murder but suspected of another twenty one. He suffered from a bipolar disorder, abused alcohol, amphetamines, marijuana, opioids, and was said to have an IQ of eighty. He lost his twin sister Tammy to meningitis at a young age, which he also contracted, and was molested by family friend with the consent of his mother.

Tommy would tell me up front he would not be able to write me without help, he couldn't afford it. We also talked about a recent 48 Hours documentary on him where he claims they filmed over three hundred hours for it.

Our correspondence accumulated one letter. Tommy was executed on April 3rd in 2014 at the age of forty nine by lethal injection.

Texas no longer lets inmates pick a final meal so Tommy had to eat what everyone else did that day: BBQ chopped brisket, chilled pasta salad, peas and carrots, sliced pickles, sliced bread, and a choice of punch, tea, or water. Tommy declined to make a final statement.

Pamela Smart is a female temptress who was convicted of being an accomplice to first degree murder as well as conspiracy to commit murder. Using her feminine ways she convinced William Flynn to murder her husband. William in turn recruited his friends Raymond Fowler, Vance Lattime, and Patrick Randall to help him.

Due to her high profile status Pamela was transferred from New Hampshire Department of Corrections to the New York Department of Corrections. In October 1996 Pamela was beaten so severely by two inmates that a plastic plate had to be inserted in the left side of her face.

Pamela would tell me she received a hate letter from a woman in Concord, Massachusetts. She also claimed to have received many offers to write a book on her case but stated, "at this time it is not appropriate."

She was unaware of Jennifer Furio's book however, Letters From Prison: Voices Of Women Murderers. When I told her, she asked if I would send her a copy of the chapter written on her.

Pamela was constantly working to improve herself telling me she was enrolled in two Master's Degree programs. If she would gain her freedom Pamela wanted to be an attorney and work on death penalty cases.

Our correspondence accumulated five letters.

In 2004 Pamela filed a lawsuit claiming the guards were sexually harassing and assaulting her. The state of New York would award Pamela twenty three thousand eight hundred seventy five dollars in November of 2009.

I have some strong views on the Pamela Smart case. I really feel she was railroaded. She received a life sentence without a chance for parole. This seems harsh for someone that didn't actually commit a murder. I am in no way defending her, she was an evil manipulative woman. But she did not pull the trigger, and the person who did and those that assisted have all been paroled.

Emanuel Webb is a serial killer who is African American and was convicted of one murder in Georgia and was paroled only to be convicted of three more murders in Connecticut after DNA connected him to four more victims.

The most noticeable thing about Emanuel's letters to me, was his state of paranoia. I expect some distrust honestly but he was all over the place. At one time he stated my letter smelled of perfume and another time asked if I was gay or straight. He appeared to be pouring the macho attitude on a bit too much.

He constantly questioned why I would write him and more specifically an alleged serial killer when all his friends had abandoned him. Emanuel claimed to be religious and to have been that way before prison, again always on the defensive.

Our correspondence accumulated two letters.

"I don't feel guilty for anything. I feel sorry for people who feel guilt."
Ted Bundy

XXXIII.

By 2010 my correspondences were dwindling and I guess honestly I just needed a break from it. I had hoped my career would have taken off by now, but it hadn't, at least not in the direction I was hoping.

I had accepted the fact I wasn't going to be a criminal profiler for the F.B.I., after all how many people truly have a shot at that. I began to think more realistically. I had tried to find a true crime author to co-write a book with as I wasn't as confident as I should have been to do it myself. I had attended book signings and reached out through email to such authors as Keith Ablow, Roderick Anscombe, Alex Beam, Philip Carlo, Stephen Michaud, Robert Mladinich, John Philpin, Fred Rosen, and Ann Rule. Unfortunately I always hit road blocks and felt maybe this was as far as I was meant to get.

I never lost interest with my subjects, just the struggle to show the world what I had learned. So from Wesley Shermantine's last letter in February 2010 until the year 2017 I was on hiatus from my writing.

I refocused myself, came up with new more realistic goals and built my confidence up until I felt the time had come for me to write this book on my own.

As I was coming up with an outline for the book I also made the decision to start writing to inmates again. Thus began the second half of my career.

"It's time. I want the killing to stop…I'm either getting six life sentences or the electric chair."

Gary Ray Bowles

XXXIV.

Chad Curtis is a former professional baseball player convicted of sexually assaulting three underage girls at Lakewood High School in Lake Odessa, Michigan.

He was drafted out of Grand Canyon University in the 1989 MLB Draft by the California Angels in the forty fifth round with the one thousandth one hundred fifty fifth pick. He would play three seasons for them, then play one and a half for the Detroit Tigers, a half for the Los Angeles Dodgers, a half for the Cleveland Indians, two and a half for the New York Yankees, and two for the Texas Rangers, appearing in one thousand two hundred and four games.

Chad played outfield and recorded one thousand sixty one hits, one hundred one homeruns, one hundred ninety five doubles, sixteen triples, and four hundred sixty one runs batted in in his MLB career. He would also win two World Series with the New York Yankees in 1998 and 1999 and earn twelve million eight hundred seventy nine thousand dollars while playing.

Chad was most proud of the fact that he has maintained relations with all six of his children and wife despite his incarceration. He stayed active by participating in a weightlifting routine and kept his faith by leading a bible study group.

Our correspondence was in July 2017 accumulated one letter.

Gary Ray Bowles is a serial killer who was convicted of three murders but suspected of six murders. He was by definition a homosexual who preyed on gay men. His father died six months before he was born leaving Gary to be physically abused by a stepfather. His murders would lead him to be added to the F.B.I.'s Ten Most Wanted List.

Starting with Gary this may represent the toughest section of this book for me. He becomes the first subject I will talk about that I am currently writing. There is a sense of loyalty that I feel like I am betraying. We are friends after all. The others I have written about were friends to, but due to whatever the circumstances, we are not anymore, and haven't been in years.

I hope if or when my current friends read this they don't take offense to anything or end our friendship over it. For the most part I am letting the world see them for who they really are. If they present themselves as a monster or sociopath to me, then that is what I have described. If they are friendly and we just discuss everyday things, then that is what I talk about. Either way, you the reader, or myself the writer, have learned something.

I also find myself obtaining more letters from respected murderabilia dealers at this time. Something I am not fond of doing, but the frustration of so many unanswered letters, and the desire to have the most information for use in this book were too much.

Gary would ask me right off the bat if I'm into women or men. He wanted to make sure I knew he killed who he believed to be child molesters, and that he really wasn't gay, having had three girlfriends in his twenty one years of incarceration. One of which he would send me a picture of from one of their visits. Tragically she would take her own life. Currently he was talking to a married girl in Texas who wanted to visit.

Gary would tell me how Victoria Redstall from The Killer Speaks misrepresented him in a documentary. Yet he kept a picture of the two of them which he sent to me and asked me to make copies of. I would make three copies for him.

Gary followed the Chicago Bears in professional football, the Chicago Bulls in professional basketball, and the Chicago Cubs in professional baseball. The later he claimed to have seen many times in person as a child.

For music Gary loved Ozzy Osbourne and Black Sabbath and even did artwork for a band in Europe. His artwork would become my most prized pieces. First I would receive a handmade Christmas card which was beautiful. Then I would receive a drawing of a dragon. Done in pencil the detail was amazing.

At this point I had changed my stance on paying for artwork and would give Gary some money for his work and time.

Our correspondence started in August 2017 and has accumulated sixteen letters and one email. He would become the third inmate I received email from.

At this time Gary has been dealing with some nagging health issues that involved minor surgery. His appeals are pushing into the final stages as well and he fears his execution could be nearing. If this happens he would be only the second person to be executed while we were still corresponding, the other being Michael Ross.

Gary has revealed a lot about himself to me and if he ever did ask me to be there for him as a witness I would.

Thomas Payne is a former professional basketball player and professional boxer who is African American and was convicted of multiple rapes.

Tom became the first African American ever to play basketball at the University of Kentucky. Due to the beginning of his criminal behavior he would leave Kentucky early and enter the NBA's first ever supplemental draft in 1971 to be drafted by the Atlanta Hawks in the first round with the second pick. He would play one season for them appearing in twenty nine games.

Tom played center and recorded one hundred nineteen points, sixty nine rebounds, and fifteen assists in his NBA career.

After the NBA Tom served time in prison then attempted a comeback upon release in the Continental Basketball Association with the Louisville Catbirds. When this failed Tom became a professional boxer.

He was a heavyweight who appeared in four fights compiling a 2-2 career record with two knockouts.

Interestingly enough Tom also attempted an acting career with a McDonald's commercial and a brief part on the eighties comedy Night Court to his credit.

Tom was very appreciative for my kind words towards his athletic achievements and would send me inspirational quotes with each letter along with a picture of him from his playing days in college which he would sign on the back. He also used meditation to help him through the days and credited his brothers for being loyal to him.

Tom followed the Florida State Seminoles, Michigan Wolverines, and Ohio State Buckeyes in college football, as well as the Carolina Panthers, New England Patriots, and Tampa Bay Buccaneers in professional football. Surprisingly he did not follow the Kentucky Wildcats in college basketball, but remains in contact and friends with an old teammate. In professional basketball he followed LeBron James due to his on and off the court actions.

Our correspondence went from August 2017 until January 2018 accumulating four letters.

Gary Ray Bowles

"The only thing that could satisfy her womanly vengeance was the life of the one that had, for an instant, taken her place."

David Graham

XXXV.

Dana Sue Gray is a female serial killer who was convicted of three murders. As a child her parents got divorced when she was just two. Growing up Dana became an adrenaline junkie with extreme spending habits who would get into relationships with men that could feed her addictions.

Dana participated in skydiving and windsurfing to satisfy her need for excitement. But when there were no men around she would rob and kill elderly women to support her need to shop. Not surprisingly Dana would constantly ask me for money. I would not give her any, and that would ultimately lead her to stop writing me. Before that happened we managed to talk about Dana's art, specifically painting. She was into impressionistic and surrealism yet would tell me her last two pieces were erotica. I would receive a card from her in which the art on it was a copy of a painting she had done. I would also receive email from her, making her the first inmate I had received email from. This was done through the JPAY website. A website created for correctional services. Dana also loved music and Led Zeppelin was her favorite.

Our correspondence went from September 2017 until November 2017 accumulating three letters and two emails.

Eric Houston is a mass killer and school shooter who was convicted of four murders and ten attempted murders.

The most memorable thing about Eric was his art. Every envelope was drawn on. His drawings remind you instantly of The Far Side by Gary Larsen. Eric even asked my help in obtaining one of his books as it was the only one he needed to complete the collection.

For music Eric enjoyed AC/DC, David Bowie, and Tom Petty, but hated our President Donald Trump. He made a few jokes around him in his art, one of which was on an envelope. I warned him he may get himself into trouble doing that. He then mentioned he had already been visited by government agents after Columbine asking if he was ever online with them.

Our correspondence went from September 2017 until March 2018 accumulating nine letters.

David Graham was convicted of murdering Adrianne Jessica Jones. David's lover Diane Zamora was also convicted of the murder. This was a dream case for the Lifetime Network. It had it all.

David was a cadet at the United States Air Force Academy in Colorado Springs, Colorado and Diane was a midshipman at the United States Naval Academy in Annapolis, Maryland. Diane was furious over an alleged affair between David and Adrianne. She convinced David that the only way to make things right was to kill her. The details became a he said versus she said. But the constant fact was both were present at the murder.

The crime happened before they both left for their colleges and appealed to me personally as I had wanted to attend the United States Military Academy in West Point, New York.

David was friendly enough, apologizing for the long wait in his response. It was about three months I had waited, and honestly given up on hearing from him.

He talked about being a minister at his facility and how long it took to get to that point. He also had just finished reading Game Of Thrones by George R.R. Martin and found much of it "obscene". Fantasy novels were his favorites to read and David planned on reading some Terry Brooks novels next.

To stay in shape he would play basketball when he could.

Our correspondence was in October 2017 accumulating one letter.

> "I have an obsession with the unattainable and I have to eliminate that I cannot attain."
>
> Robert John Bardo

XXXVI.

Michael Terry is a serial killer who is African American and was convicted of two murders but suspected of four others. The murders were of men and homosexual by nature.

Michael would deny murdering the men to me and honestly by this point in my life I had seen many innocent people in prison. I can't judge, I haven't seen the evidence, etc… But I find myself helping more now than before.

I would give "Big Mike", as he liked to be called, the contact information of many different inmate innocence groups for them to decide. Michael claimed there were only three computers available for inmates to use even though the facility housed seventeen hundred inmates. To help him get through the day he would read from the Bible.

Our correspondence started in December 2017 and has accumulated fourteen letters.

John Wesley Wilson, "Teddy", is a former professional football player who is African American and was convicted of multiple drug charges as well as a firearm charge.

He was drafted out of the University of Central Florida in the 1987 NFL Draft by the Washington Redskins in the tenth round with the two hundred seventy fourth pick, becoming the first University of Central Florida player to be drafted by an NFL team. He would play part of one season for them appearing in three games.

John played wide receiver and recorded five receptions, one hundred twelve yards receiving, and two touchdowns receiving in his NFL career. His time with the Redskins was during one of the two times the NFL players went on strike. This season, the second of the strikes, the NFL would use scab players. This was made famous by the movie The Replacements in 2000. They would play three games before the strike ended, winning all three, and held the distinction of being the only team that had no players cross the picket line. This played a major role in the Redskins winning Super Bowl XXII over the Denver Broncos.

John resurfaced in the World League of American Football with the Birmingham Fire playing one season while appearing in seven games and recording three receptions and twenty eight yards receiving in his WLAF career.

Much like all the previous athletes I've written, John was very gracious for my kind words regarding his playing days and signed a letter Teddy Wilson Washington Redskins #80 as did Darion Conner with his team and number. He would also become someone I would send more legal information to so he could pursue his innocence claims.

He was proud to tell me the Redskins were finally going to honor those scab players that contributed to the 1987 Super Bowl run by presenting them with their long overdue championship rings. I would bring up the new 30 For 30 documentary, Year Of The Scab, asking if he had seen it. John had been approached about participating in it but said his lawyers advised against it. He regrets that decision now.

Our correspondence started in December of 2017 and has accumulated eight letters and twenty four emails. John became the second inmate to send me email. In one of those emails John shares his hopes that someday we could meet and have a few drinks, maybe even see a Redskins game together.

Robert John Bardo was convicted of the murder of actress Rebecca Schaeffer. He was diagnosed with manic depression and had a history of stalking women leading up to this murder. While in prison John was stabbed eleven times by another inmate in 2007. He was fortunate enough to survive.

Robert's letters reminded me of Eric Houston's a lot. They contained lots of jumbled thoughts randomly placed in different areas of the letter. It would often take several reads to understand. He would also put some of these thoughts on the envelope, both sides. It was like he was thinking aloud.

Robert explained a petition he had started for gun ammo shortage and hoped I could forward it along. Interestingly enough it was a unique idea. All cities, states, and police agencies would buy all the ammo on the market thus creating a shortage.

I initially wrote Robert hoping to acquire some of his drawings of other famous killers, specifically serial killers. He stated he did not do those anymore. He had previously done ones of Jeffrey Dahmer, Albert Fish, John Wayne Gacy, Ed Gein, Gary Heidnik, Edmund Kemper, Charles Manson, and Dennis Rader. Alarmingly he also did drawings of Rebecca Schaeffer his victim. Now Robert spends most of his time drawing celebrities and musicians along with participating in self-help groups.

In a twist of irony he would ask me why I had a fascination with serial killers, informing me that many killers idolized other killers, as he had done with Mark David Chapman, the killer of John Lennon. Next he would mention the capture of "The Golden State Killer" and that he had just watched a Dateline episode entitled "Best Friend Until Death". But I'm the one fascinated?

He would go on to ask me a list of eight questions that again were so random and bizarre. One of which was, "what intimate acts does Stormy Daniels do in her adult movies?". Another was "what year was the Richard Gere gerbil in the rear rumor?".

Our correspondence went from April 2018 until July 2018 accumulating four letters.

"I would suggest that when a person has a thought of doing anything serious against the law, that before they did that they should go to a quiet place and think about it seriously."

William Bonin

XXXVII.

These individuals in the next chapters are killers whose letters were written to other people. I obtained them from murderabilia dealers. I did not write these killers personally or I may have tried but never received a response. However, I felt I needed to acquire samples of their writings even if they were deceased, not interested in answering me, or I felt they wouldn't answer. Plus it gave me a different perspective depending on the personality of the writer.

Richard Angelo is a serial killer and an angel of death who was convicted of four murders at varying degrees but suspected in several more. His legal team stated he had dissociative identity disorder but the jury wasn't convinced.

Richard's letter was to a woman named Ms. Miller and most of it was spent apologizing to her that a fellow inmate, whom he thought was a friend, took her address from him with the intention of writing her.

He would express his fondness for reading fantasy, historical, and science fiction novels. Richard also liked to draw and enjoyed listening to the Beatles and Pink Floyd.

This letter was written in November 1994.

William Bonin, "The Freeway Killer", was a serial killer who was convicted of fourteen murders but suspected of many more. He was a homosexual Air Force veteran who was both physically and sexually abused as a child and whose alcoholic father died when he was only fourteen. William's grandfather was a convicted child molester.

He recruited several young men to aid him in his crimes. They were Vernon Butts, Gregory Miley, and James Munro. Vernon Butts would hang himself in his cell on January 11th in 1981 while awaiting trial, Gregory Miley was said to have an IQ of fifty six, and James Munro I would later acquire a letter written by him.

William's letters were written to two different murderabila dealers. The first letter was to Kregg Sanders, and the second was to Rick Stanton.

William had enclosed art with Rick's letter, but did not state what it was. He would also try to sell four books he had written to Kregg Sanders. Two were books of short stories. He was asking for twenty five dollars for those. One was a science fiction novel entitled Missing Time. It was two hundred thirty four pages and he was asking for forty dollars for that one. Lastly was an adventure novel entitled CB And Company. It was one hundred fifty two pages and he was asking for twenty five dollars for that one.

William would ask Kregg to exchange pictures. A lot of these prison photos will end up on murderabilia sites.

These letters were written in November 1993 and December 1993. William was executed on February 23rd in 1996 at the age of forty nine by lethal injection.

His last meal consisted of two large pizzas, three pints of ice cream and three six packs of Coke. His last words were, "I felt the death penalty is not an answer to the problems at hand. I feel it sends the wrong message to the people of this country. Young people act as they see other people acting instead of as people tell them to act.".

Harvey Carignan, "The Want-Ad Killer", is a serial killer who was convicted of one murder while in the Army, and despite a sentence to hang, was paroled after eleven years only to be convicted of two more murders but was suspected in many more. He was a chronic bedwetter who had been diagnosed with chorea, a neurological disorder that causes involuntary movements in the body.

Harvey made claims of sexual abuse suffered at the hands of a babysitter and again while in reform school. He had the distinction of serving eight years of his first murder conviction at Alcatraz Federal Penitentiary.

On a website SKCentral.com ran by Joe Hiles, a posted questionnaire completed by Harvey states he had three kids, all having died tragically, one from cancer, one from a drug overdose, and another from a gunshot.

Harvey's letter was written to Mike and Sharon, whom he acknowledged as two of his most trusted friends along with an active F.B.I. agent and an ex police officer from Alabama. The later two seem ironic as Harvey views "police officers and F.B.I. agents as slime".

In his letter he also mentions the famous Chicago mass killer Richard Speck. He was responsible for the murders of eight student nurses back in 1966. Richard died in prison on December 5th in 1991, one day short of his fiftieth birthday from a heart attack.

This letter was written in June 1996.

"Yes, I did it, but I'm a sick man and can't be judged by the standards of other men."

Juan Corona

XXXVIII.

Daniel Conahan, "The Hog Trail Killer", is a serial killer who was convicted of one murder but suspected of many more. He was a homosexual Navy veteran working as a nurse.

Daniel's letter was written to another famous murderabilia dealer Ken Karnig, who runs Supernaught.com. He thanked Ken for sending him paper and stamps. Daniel would ask Ken, "I'd like to hear about your sex life".

This letter was written in May 2000.

Juan Corona was a serial killer who was Latino and was convicted of twenty five murders. He was homosexual and suffered from schizophrenia. Juan would set the United States record for murder convictions. His record would last only two years until 1973 when Dean Corll and his accomplices would break that record with a mark of twenty eight.

While in prison at the California Medical Facility in Vacaville Juan was stabbed thirty two times by a group of inmates on December 6th in 1973. He would again survive another attack years later at Corcoran State Prison where he would nearly lose an eye. Juan would suffer from dementia in the later years and was denied parole eight times over the years.

Juan's letter was also to Ken Karnig. Ken had apparently sent him pictures.

Juan thanked him for them. His writing was very sloppy for a man whose IQ was one hundred thirty.

This letter was written in April 2001. Juan died in prison on March 4th in 2019 at the age of eighty five.

Colin Ferguson is a mass killer who is African American and was convicted of six murders and nineteen attempted murders. Colin was highly intelligent, having studied at Nassau Community College as a dean's list student, then at Adelphi University majoring in business administration. Unfortunately his views on life, politics, and racism would keep him from finishing any of his schooling. His trial would become a media circus as Colin defended himself.

While in prison in March of 1994 Ferguson would be attacked by several inmates and receive a broken nose and a black eye. As I previously mentioned, also in 1994, Colin would have a physical altercation with serial killer Joel Rifkin in prison.

Right out of a Saturday Night Live skit it sounded like this: Ferguson: "Be quiet I'm on the phone." Rifkin: Ignores Ferguson. Ferguson: Escalates…"I wiped out six devils, and you only killed women." Rifkin: "Yeah, but I had more victims." Ferguson: Punches Rifkin.

Colin's letter was written to Michael. He thanked him for sending twenty dollars. He also apologized for his letter being so short due to him spending his time working on an upcoming appeal. Colin promised a longer letter next time.

This letter was written in December 1997.

John Wayne Gacy was a serial killer I previously mentioned and acknowledged having acquired three letters he wrote. He would pass Dean Corll's twenty eight murder convictions to set the United States record at thirty three. His record would last for over twenty years until Gary Leon Ridgway, "The Green River Killer", would pass him with forty nine convictions.

One of his letters I have was written to Sondra London, she was famous for authoring Killer Fiction along with serial killer Gerald Schaefer, and The Making Of A Serial Killer along with serial killer and fiancé Danny Rolling. She would then author True Vampires and have French killer Nicolas Claux illustrate it.

"I can honestly tell you, and I'm not bragging, if I had a problem with girls, it's not because I didn't have enough. It is because I had too many."

Gerald Gallego

XXXIX.

Gerald Gallego, "The Sex Slave Killer", was a serial killer who was convicted of murders in both California and Nevada. His wife Charlene was an accomplice for these crimes.

He grew up in a home were his mother worked as a prostitute and his father was executed in the gas chamber at Mississippi State Penitentiary when Gerald was only nine for murdering a police officer.

Gerald would sexually abuse his first victim when he was only thirteen. The victim was only six. By the time of his capture he had piled up twenty three arrests and seven marriages.

Gerald's letter was written to Phyllis. He tells her she is the only woman he has answered since he has been incarcerated. The reason being is he didn't want to have to say goodbye one day when his execution came up. As it was he couldn't face himself in a mirror. He then tells her she is "so very beautiful", as she has sent him pictures of herself.

This letter was written in August 1992. Gerald died in prison on July 18th in 2002 at the age of fifty six from rectal cancer. Charlene Gallego was released from prison in July 1997.

Robin Gecht is one fourth of "The Chicago Rippers", a cannibalistic cult he led that were suspected of up to eighteen murders. He had at one time worked for fellow serial killer John Wayne Gacy. His partners in murder were brothers Andrew and Thomas Kokoraleis along with Edward Spreitzer. The group was known for removing breasts of the women they killed.

Robin's letter was written to Liz and included a "surprise" with it. Robin stated that he had "to loose the tummy" which leads me to believe he sent her a picture. Possibly a shirtless one. He stated "lack of sex" was to blame for the tummy.

This letter was written in June 1997. Andrew Kokoraleis was executed on March 17th in 1999 at the age of thirty seven by lethal injection.

Jeremy Jones is a serial killer who was suspected in as many as twenty one murders. He once stated he could "talk the panties off a nun".

Jeremy's letter was written to Kerry. It also is one of the most revolting letters I have read. In it he brags about the size of his penis constantly and what an unbelievable lover he is. Strangely he refers to the size of his penis in centimeters and not inches. Twenty five centimeters to be exact. This translates to almost ten inches.

He tells Kerry he loves her and wants to marry her. He also asks her to send sexy pictures of herself.

There is no date on his letter.

Eugene McWatters is a serial killer who was convicted of three murders. He abused alcohol and drugs and found his victims through them.

Eugene's letter was written to Joe. I believe this was Joe Hiles. He apologized for not having written sooner as he hurt his hand playing basketball and has been unable to write.

Joe had sent Eugene some short stories he had written and Eugene stated he would write his mother and ask her to send him some of the short stories he had written. He would then in turn send them to Joe.

There is no date on this letter.

Envelopes from Christa Pike, the youngest female ever sentenced to death at the age of 18

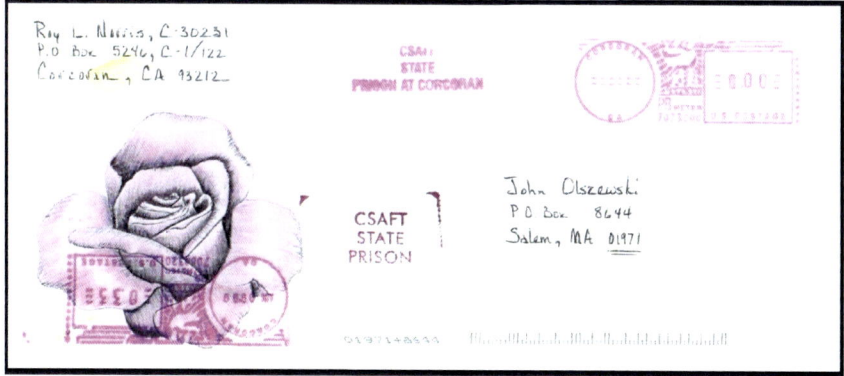

Envelope from serial killer Roy Norris

Envelopes from serial killer Hadden Clark

Envelopes from serial killer Hadden Clark

Envelope from serial killer Hadden Clark

Envelope from Tina Cornelius who killed her two young children

Envelope from serial killer Phillip Jablonski

Card made by serial killer Gary Ray Bowles

Serial killer Randall Woodfield with chess set he made

Leatherwork by Randall Woodfield

Serial killer Dayton Leroy Rogers

Former NFL player Ramsey Dardar (on far left)

KENNETH BIANCHI

THEODORE BUNDY

ANGELO BUONO

ALBERT FISH

JOHN WAYNE GACY

EDWARD GEIN

EDMUND KEMPER

BOBBY JOE LONG

CLIFFORD OLSON

Serial killer trading cards

Serial killer comic books

"I saw the light over the confessional and the voice said: That's the person to kill."

Herbert Mullin

XXXX.

Bruce Mendenhall is a serial killer who was suspected in numerous murders in multiple states. Bruce is one of the many recent serial killers who makes his living as a long haul trucker. According to the F.B.I. there are currently twenty five in prison, including Oscar Ray Bolin, Keith Jesperson, and Ward Weaver Jr. whom I've already discussed, and Adam Lane and Robert Rhoades whom I will be discussing in upcoming chapters. Other serial killer truck drivers that I don't mention in this book are John Wayne Boyer, Wayne Adam Ford, Dellmus Colvin, and Edward Surratt.

The F.B.I. has taken this trend so seriously that they created the Highway Serial Killings Initiative. Most everyone reading this is probably familiar with VICAP, (Violent Criminal Apprehension Program), made famous by shows like Criminal Minds.

The quick summary is information, in particular, signatures of murders are put into a database which can match similar murders throughout the country to indicate possible serial killers.

The Highway Serial Killings Initiative is even more specific. Murders that occurred in and around truck routes and stops are put in a database as are a list of truckers with violent criminal backgrounds. This has already helped local law enforcement agencies immensely.

According to the F.B.I. around four decades ago thirty percent of the serial killers in our country were getting away with at least five murders, now they state only thirteen percent do, and close to half are caught after just two murders. This is due to advances in forensics and police procedures.

With that being said it seems a high percentage of those serial killers who are still successful, five or more victims, appear to be truck drivers. Keep in mind to, the F.B.I. believes that at any given time there is between thirty five to fifty serial killers roaming our country.

Given the F.B.I.'s implications with the Highway Serial Killings Initiative would it be safe to say of that thirty five to fifty, maybe five to ten are truck drivers?

Bruce's letter was written to Eric. He asks him to send word puzzle books if he can. He also claims to read four hundred pages a day and that CBS News reporter Nick Beres had evidence and didn't say anything.

Eric had recently been having dental problems as Bruce stated he can relate to them as he had a tooth pulled before.

This letter was written in November 2010.

Herbert Mullin is a serial killer who was convicted of eleven murders but suspected of thirteen. He was a paranoid schizophrenic who abused LSD. He believed his murders were preventing a major earthquake.

Herbert's letter was written to Ken. I believe this to be Ken Karnig. The letter was short and extremely telling. It consisted of all numbers. The first part was stating the time between the first fourth of July, 1776, and the upcoming fourth of July, 2017. He states two hundred forty one years which is correct. But after this he is wrong on the other calculations. He states that there have been eighty eight thousand twenty seven days, two million one hundred twelve thousand six hundred forty eight hours, one hundred twenty six million seven hundred fifty eight thousand eight hundred eighty minutes, and lastly seven billion six hundred five million five hundred thirty two thousand eight hundred seconds.

I assumed it to be right but as I wrote this I decided to check. The numbers are off. I even did it to the date the letter was written, June 27, and they don't match to that date either.

He also added a complex math question at the end of the letter. I felt his letter was something I would have received from Ted Kaczynski, "The Unabomber", as he was the mathematical genius.

This letter was written in June 2017. Over the years Herbert has been denied parole at least ten times.

James Munro is a serial killer who was mentioned before as an accomplice to William Bonin.

James's letter was written to Ken. This is probably Ken Karnig again. In the letter James asks Ken for money and states he has all of William Bonin's court transcripts.

The implication is obvious. For the right amount James is willing to sell them.

This letter was written in June 1996.

> "The name penitentiary came from the word penitent – and you learn how to be penitent in prison."
>
> James Riva

XXXXI.

James Riva is a local killer and cannibal who had spent time in a mental hospital and who was convicted of murdering his grandmother. He believed himself to be a vampire who was seven hundred years old. He would drink his grandmother's blood from the bullet holes he had put into her.

James's letter was written to Jeremy. He mentions a drawing he did for him as well as officers harassing him. James talks about keeping in shape by going to the weight room three nights a week.

This letter was written in March 2013.

Glen Rogers, "The Cross Country Killer", is a serial killer who was convicted of two murders but suspected of many more. One of those others is Nicole Brown Simpson, the wife of former professional football player O.J. Simpson, who went on trial for her murder, but was acquitted. This is a theory I don't believe in. Glen would however make the F.B.I.'s Ten Most Wanted List due to his other crimes. His IQ was said to only be seventy six.

Glen's letter was written to Ken. This again is probably Ken Karnig. He states he has been calling but Ken is never home. He also enclosed legal paperwork which he expects Ken to hide porn pictures in. Glen asks them to be placed in the middle of the documents then staple the documents together.

Lastly he talked about a girl named Lynn visiting him. He states she "had some big tits".

This letter had no date.

George Russell is a serial killer who is African American and was convicted of three murders. He suffered from a condition called piquerism. A person with this derives sexual pleasure from the penetration of skin. We know this because one of his victims had two hundred thirty one small knife wounds.

George's letter was written to Jessi. It was very neatly written but he is very skeptical as to why she wrote him and asks her, "have you ever written to anyone in prison?".

He does open up however and talks about being born in West Palm Beach and exchanging photos. Jessi had mentioned doing glass blowing in college while George states he doesn't consider that art, his art is poems and short stories which he writes.

This letter was written in February 2004.

"I've done something foolish. You're going to be mad at me."
Gerard Schaefer

XXXXII.

Gerard Schaefer was a serial killer who was convicted of two murders but suspected of many more. He had tortured animals as a child before working his way up to attending Florida Atlantic University and becoming a police officer.

Gerard's letter was written to Phyllis. I previously mentioned Gerald Gallego having written to a Phyllis. I don't find Phyllis to be that common of a name and suspect it is the same woman, or maybe even a dealer pretending to be a woman.

Both letters seem similar in that both killers are extremely interested in a future with their Phyllis.

What makes me think that this Phyllis at least is a dealer is the questions she must have asked. They were concerning fellow serial killers Ted Bundy and Gerald Stano, both of whom he did time with at that prison. This would drive up the value of the letters.

Gerard states Gerald Stano "hates women passionately". Gerard then goes on to say "women are emotional creatures, men are rational creatures".

He also talked about the change of seasons and about marrying Phyllis. Then the letter takes a change as he gets controlling.

Gerard begins questioning Phyllis's eating. He then asks her the last time she has had an enema. If she hasn't he encourages her to get one.

Lastly Gerard talks about his semen production. He claims it is due to lack of sex. He refuses to engage in homosexual sex even though it goes on a lot at his prison.

This letter was written in June 1993. While in prison Gerard would become involved with Sondra London as I mentioned previously. He would also sue author Michael Newton and F.B.I. agent Robert Ressler before being murdered by another inmate, Vincent Rivera, on December 3rd 1995 at the age of forty nine.

Robert Benjamin Smith is a mass killer who was convicted of five murders as well as two attempted murders. He was only eighteen and had spent much of his teen years moving around due to his father's job. As a result of this he had difficulty forming friendships and had been isolating and reading books on famous killers. Just months before his crimes, were those of Richard Speck, the killing of eight nurses, and Charles Whitman, the killing of nineteen people on the University of Texas campus. Robert chose the Rose-Mar College of Beauty in Mesa, Arizona as the site of his massacre.

Robert's letter was written to Mr. Sanders. This is probably Kregg Sanders. I believe this because of Robert's statements about a novel and getting it to Kregg.

Unfortunately he feels his contact has thrown away the manuscript. Due to this Robert doesn't want it brought up again and feels "his spirits are at such a low ebb".

This letter was written in December 1995.

Gerald Stano was a serial killer who was convicted of one murder but at one time confessed to forty one, while law enforcement think the totals could be higher. He would recant the confessions later. He was an adopted bedwetter who was so neglected as a baby he was said to have survived by eating his own feces.

Gerald's letter was written to James. In it he asks for twenty dollars and apologizes for the delay in answering his letter as he has been working on his case.

He also states he is waiting for James to be approved on his list. I would assume it is either for a phone call or a visit.

This letter was written in May 1995. Gerald was executed on March 23rd in 1998 at the age of forty six in the electric chair.

His last meal consisted of a Delmonico steak, baked potato, salad, lima beans, two liters of Pepsi, and a half gallon of mint chocolate chip ice cream. His last words were: "I am innocent. I am frightened. I was threatened and I was held month after month without any real legal representation. I confessed to crimes I did not commit."

"Human life holds very little meaning for me as anyone can kill or be killed."
David Paul Hammer

XXXXIII.

This chapter will deal with other individuals I corresponded with but over the years have taken them out of my research. The reasons I took them out varied from them not being murderers or if they were, not being famous enough.

In all there have been fifteen removed from my research. I have decided to briefly mention nine of them because they were murderers.

The first I will talk about is Clyde Blacks. I found his address on a death penalty website. He was on death row in Trinidad & Tobago. I never could find any information on him or his crime online however. This was the major reason I removed him. I think at the time he told me that he killed a man in a drunken bar fight. The thing that stood out to me was the letters he wrote were folded into the envelope and had all tropical air male themes.

Kristina Burris is a female killer who was convicted of murdering her mother. Her case had some controversy and she would eventually win her freedom while we were corresponding. We would lose touch after she was released to a halfway house.

Joseph Copeland would tell me he was convicted of murdering a drug dealer. Now when I try to find information on him I can't, I believe at the time I did verify it.

I met Joseph through The College Guild. I volunteered for them to grade inmate work for correspondence courses.

Peter Dushame was a unique case. He had been involved in two separate car accidents in which people died. He then drank chronically and was arrested for multiple drunk driving offenses, the last one taking the life of a ten year old girl.

He would help set up and run substance abuse programs at his prison and even sent me a copy of the curriculum.

James Hairston was convicted of a double murder along with an accomplice in a robbery. He is on death row in Idaho. I ended up writing him because I initially wrote to serial killer James Wood, he didn't answer but instead gave my letter to James who was looking for a pen pal.

This was the second time this happened to me. Years before I had attempted to start a correspondence with Kenneth Bianchi, one of "The Hillside Stranglers". Instead I received a letter from another inmate he gave my letter to.

James was good at drawing and even though I removed him from my research I kept and framed a card he drew for me. It was of a wolf and was so good that I often showcased it during my lecture, Imprisoned Artists: The Art Of Famous Murderers.

David Paul Hammer was convicted of murdering his cellmate in federal prison to earn himself the death penalty. He had grown up experiencing physical and sexual abuse to a life of drug abuse.

While in prison he became close friends with Timothy McVeigh, the man responsible for the Oklahoma City bombing. David has published numerous books, including two on Timothy McVeigh, Secrets Worth Dying For and Deadly

Secrets.

Soon to be sixty David has spent forty years in prison including an unbelievable thirty in solitary confinement and sixteen on death row.

Brenda Medina is a female killer who is Latino and was convicted of a gang murder for the Las Solidas out of Connecticut. She was only seventeen at the time of the murder and I had read about her in Wally Lamb's book Couldn't Keep It To Myself: Testimonies From Our Imprisoned Sisters.

Michael Thomas is African American and was convicted of arranging the murder of a witness from behind bars. The man was going to testify that Michael had committed a home invasion on him.

Michael received the death penalty and I ended up writing him after joining the Death Row Support Project. They randomly select an inmate who is seeking a pen pal and forward you the letter.

I hoped I might get somebody a little more famous and was a bit disappointed that in all actuality he wasn't even a murderer. We did however exchange a few letters.

I would like to add my opinion here as well. I do not believe he should have received the death penalty for this since he did not actually commit the murder. To me the case draws parallels to Pamela Smart's and her no chance at parole.

This is why I can not support the death penalty, it is applied unfairly. How can someone who didn't commit the murder receive the death penalty while the killer in the same case only received life without parole? It makes no sense.

Richard Tully was convicted of breaking into the home of a nurse and murdering her. He would stab her twenty three times and receive the death penalty for it.

    I would find him on a death penalty website. I wrote him hoping to acquire one of his paintings which were amazing. Unfortunately I never did. He would want too much for them.

Card drawn by James Hairston

"I didn't want to hurt them, I only wanted to kill them."
David Berkowitz

XXXXIV.

The following chapters will mention the many killers and professional athletes I wrote over the years who did not answer me for whatever reason.

Charles Albright, "The Eyeball Killer", is a serial killer who was convicted of one murder but suspected of three. He was adopted and killed small animals as a teenager.

His crime(s) were notorious as his victim(s) all had their eyes removed. This would aid to him being labeled a psychopath.

David Berkowitz, "The Son Of Sam", is a serial killer who was convicted of six murders while wounding another seven. He had been adopted as a child and would experience the death of his adoptive mother at fourteen. He was a fire setter before joining the Army as well.

I was really surprised he didn't answer my letter. I wrote complimenting him on his change while in prison and how he should be proud of it because it is helping others.

Whether or not the change is legit, can be debated, but I would have thought his ego would not have been able to resist the praising. I was wrong however.

David was friends with serial killer Arthur Shawcross whom I discussed earlier in the book. They were on the same unit at the Sullivan Correctional Facility in

Fallsburg, New York.

Kenneth Bianchi, one half of "The Hillside Stranglers", is a serial killer who was convicted of two murders in Washington state by himself, and was an accomplice to ten murders in California with his cousin Angelo Buono. He is also a suspect in three unsolved murders known as "The Alphabet Murders", in his hometown of Rochester, New York. This was a unique case were all the victims first and last names began with the same letter.

Ken was adopted and would experience the death of his adoptive father in his early teens. Labeled with many a diagnosis throughout his life his trial was no different. He would claim he suffered from multiple personality disorder and also be diagnosed with an antisocial personality disorder.

His legacy wouldn't end there, he got a groupie, Veronica Compton, to attack a woman in a twisted plot to kill and place his semen on her in attempt to free Ken. She had smuggled his semen out during a visit.

As stated before, Ken gave my letter to another inmate so he could write me. Angelo Buono would die in prison on September 21st in 2002 at the age of sixty seven from a heart attack.

Angelo's legacy wouldn't end either as his grandson Christopher would shoot his grandmother Mary Castillo, Angelo's ex-wife, in 2007. She survived but Christopher would kill himself shortly after.

Debra Brown is a female serial killer who along with Alton Coleman took eight lives. Both were African American and Debra had a history of head trauma as a child as well as a low IQ. One psychiatrist labeled her with a dependent personality disorder.

Alton Coleman would be labeled as having an antisocial personality disorder and being narcissistic. He would also make the F.B.I.'s Ten Most Wanted List and receive the death penalty in three different states.

Alton was executed at Southern Ohio Correctional Facility on April 26th in 2002 at the age of forty six by lethal injection.

His last meal consisted of a New York strip steak, sautéed mushrooms, sweet potato pie with whipped cream, biscuits with brown gravy, broccoli with cheese, french fries, onion rings, collard greens, fried chicken breast, green lettuce salad, corn bread, cherry coke, and butter pecan ice cream. His last words were: "The Lord is my Shepherd", over and over again.

David Carpenter, "The Trailside Killer", is a serial killer who was convicted of five murders but suspected of others. He was physically abused when young and had a history of bed wetting, stuttering, and torturing animals. He would also be locked up at age thirteen for sexually abusing his cousins.

It should be mentioned that David was at one time thought to be the "Zodiac Killer". He would be cleared however.

Bradfield Clark was previously mentioned as serial killer Hadden Clark's brother who had also been convicted of murder. He had cannibalized parts of his victim.

Richard Cottingham is a serial killer who was convicted of five murders, suspected in a sixth, and is said to have claimed over eighty five murders.

Charles Cullen is a serial killer who was an angel of death and convicted of twenty two murders, five attempted murders, and suspected in possibly hundreds more. As a child Charles's father would die when he was only seven months old, he would make his first suicide attempt at age nine, then join the Navy.

Ronald Dominique is a serial killer who was convicted of eight murders but confessed to twenty three murders. He was a homosexual who targeted other gay men.

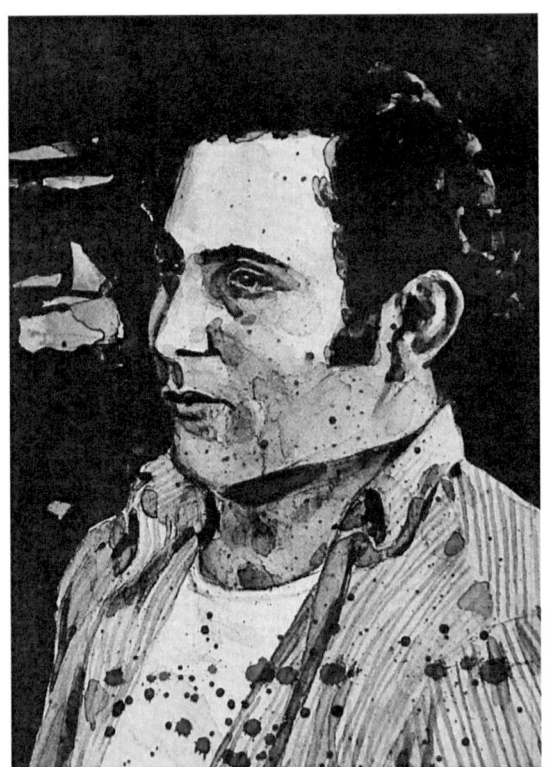

DAVID BERKOWITZ

"Going back in my life...I was...I guess what you might call very frustrated."
Robert Hansen

XXXXV.

Rod Ferrell was convicted of two murders. He was the leader of a vampire cult whose followers included Scott Anderson, Dana Cooper, and Charity Keesee, who all received varying sentences for their roles in the murders.

Rod had received several diagnoses including Asperger's syndrome and schizotypal personality disorder. I would write him to obtain some of his artwork. He was known for his drawings of other famous killers much like Robert Bardo.

Some of the killers Rod had drawn were James Holmes, the mass killer at the Colorado movie theater, and Ricky Kasso, "The Acid King", who murdered a fellow teen in a Satanic inspired killing.

One of, if not the first, true crime books I ever read was on Ricky Kasso, Say You Love Satan. He would commit suicide in jail on July 7th in 1984 at the age of seventeen.

Kristen Gilbert is a local female serial killer who was an angel of death and convicted of four murders and two attempted murders.

Sean Gillis is a serial killer who was convicted of seven murders but suspected of eight murders.

In the years before his arrest for the murder charges he had been arrested for drunk driving and also possession of marijuana.

Gwendolyn Graham is a female serial killer and an angel of death who along with her lover and partner Catherine Wood were convicted of five murders.

Robert Hansen was a serial killer who was convicted of four murders but confessed to seventeen. He had a stutter, briefly was an Army Reservist, and had served time for arson.

I found his case unique in that he would release his victims into the Alaskan wilderness and then hunt them down like wild animals.

I wrote Robert two or three times over the years but he never answered any of them.

Robert died in prison on August 21st in 2014 at the age of seventy five.

Cindy Hendy is a female serial killer who was an accomplice to David Parker Ray, "The Tool Box Killer", in his three murder convictions and possible sixty other suspected murders. David was bullied as a youth before joining the Army. He would have Cindy, who was his girlfriend, aid him along with another accomplice Dennis Roy Yancy. Before their arrest David would even involve his own daughter Glenda Jean Ray in the crimes.

David died in prison on May 28th in 2002 at the age of sixty two from a heart attack. Dennis Yancy would serve eleven years in prison for his role before being paroled only to violate his parole three months later and return to prison where he currently remains. Glenda Jean Ray served two and a half years before being paroled.

Cindy meanwhile had been scheduled for a 2017 release, but New Mexico Department of Corrections were able to keep her another two years before she was paroled on July 15th in 2019.

I feel this is a good point for me to make a statement or two concerning not only Cindy Hendy's release, but also other women's releases who were partners to their male lovers.

I feel the female half of a killing duo often gets a lighter sentence, and will get paroled at some point. Many people including the jurors feel they are a victim to.

Having studied all these cases I think I can honestly say the Caril Ann Fugate's, Charlene Gallego's, and Karla Homolka's of the world were just as evil as their male counterparts and should never have been granted parole.

Caril Ann Fugate is a female mass killer who along with her lover and partner Charles Starkweather were responsible for eleven murders. Both were teenagers at the time and Charles had a speech impediment.

Charles was executed at Nebraska State Penitentiary on June 25th in 1959 at the age of twenty in the electric chair. Caril received a life sentence yet was paroled after only seventeen and a half years.

Several movies have been made on this case including Natural Born Killers, which is loosely based on this case.

Karla Homolka is a female serial killer who along with her lover and partner Paul Bernardo were responsible for a handful of murders, one of which was Karla's own sister. They were known as the "Ken and Barbie Killers". Paul was also known as the "Scarborough Rapist" who committed over a dozen rapes. Paul's father had previously been convicted of child molestation.

Karla would be released after serving only twelve years, much to the dismay of many citizens.

This just is another example of how the court systems, and criminal justice systems fail us.

Sam Hurd is a former professional football player who is African American and was convicted of facilitating a drug ring.

He went undrafted out of Northern Illinois University in 2006 before being signed by the Dallas Cowboys who he spent five seasons for. He would play one season with the Chicago Bears next before his career ended due to his arrest. In all he played in seventy seven games.

Sam played wide receiver recording fifty three receptions seven hundred thirty nine yards receiving and two touchdowns receiving in his NFL career.

Colin Ireland was a serial killer from England who was homosexual and convicted of five murders. He never knew his father, had a history with arson, and was an Army veteran.

Colin died in prison on February 21st in 2012 at the age of fifty seven from pulmonary fibrosis.

Michael Jace was an actor who is African American and was convicted of murdering his wife. He was most known for his role as Officer Julien Lowe on the television series The Shield.

Eddie Johnson is a former professional basketball player who is African American and was convicted of sexual battery of a minor under twelve.

He was drafted out of Auburn University in the 1977 NBA Draft by the Atlanta Hawks in the third round with the forty ninth pick. He would play eight and half seasons with the Atlanta Hawks, a half season with the Cleveland Cavaliers, and a half season with the Seattle SuperSonics appearing in six hundred seventy five games.

Eddie played guard and recorded ten thousand one hundred sixty three points, three thousand four hundred thirty six assists, one thousand five hundred twenty two rebounds, seven hundred sixty one steals, and eighty nine blocks.

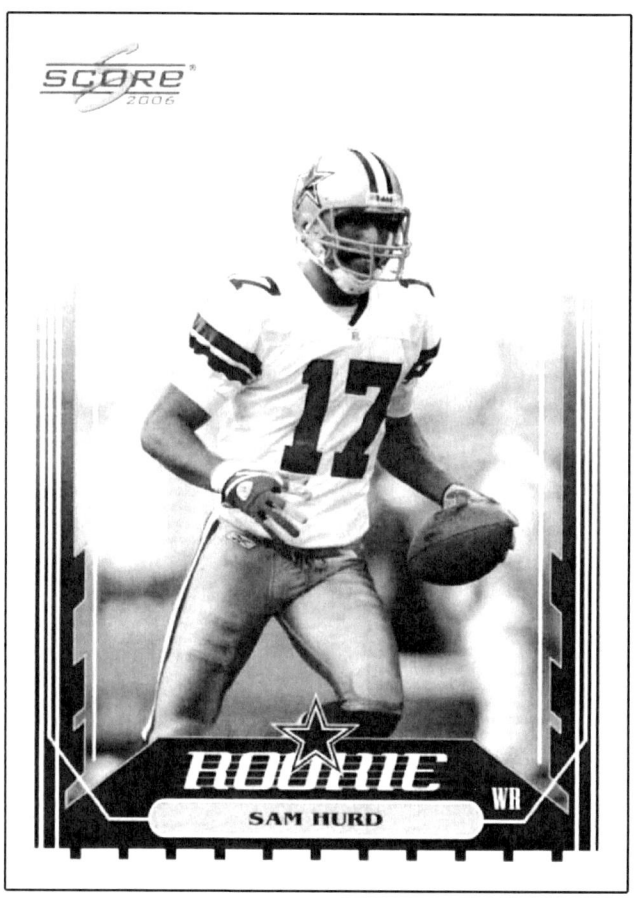

Former NFL player Sam Hurd

"One side of me says, I'd like to talk to her, date her. The other side of me says, I wonder what her head would look like on a stick?"

Edmund Kemper

XXXXVI.

Edmund Kemper, "The Co-ed Killer", is a serial killer who was convicted of two murders, those of his grandparents as a teen, before being released after six years at the age of twenty one only to murder eight more times. His second to last victim being his own mother whom he decapitated to use her head as a dart board. Her tongue and larynx were put in the garbage disposal.

In response to this Ed would say, "That seemed appropriate as much as she'd bitched and screamed and yelled at me over so many years.".

I wrote to Ed on three or four different occasions over the years but was never able to get a response. Letters from Ed are hard to come by and I can only imagine how revealing they must be considering Ed's IQ has been tested and said to be one hundred forty five, placing him at genius level. Add to this the paranoid schizophrenic diagnosis made by court psychiatrists and one should get some very interesting responses.

Roger Kibbe, "The I-5 Strangler", is a serial killer who was convicted of seven murders but suspected of eight.

Adam Leroy Lane is a serial killer who was convicted of two murders and two attempted murders, as well as being suspected in numerous others due to his extensive traveling as a truck driver.

The last attack where he was captured was in Chelmsford, Massachusetts, giving this case a local connection for me.

Michael McBain is a former professional hockey player who was convicted of sexual assault on a minor under fourteen.

He was drafted in the 1995 NHL Draft by the Tampa Bay Lightning in the second round with the thirtieth pick. He would play in parts of two seasons with them, appearing in sixty four games.

Mike played defenseman and recorded seven assists and seven points in his NHL career.

William McDonald, "The Sydney Mutilator", was a serial killer who was from Australia and convicted of four murders but admitted to five. He was a homosexual Army veteran who was raped while in the service by an officer.

Diagnosed with schizophrenia he would spend some time in a mental asylum before he begin killing men and removing their penises.

While in prison he would be transferred to a secure mental hospital. William would die there on May 12th in 2015 at the age of ninety from natural causes. He was the longest serving and oldest inmate in New South Wales.

Dexter Manley is a former professional football player who is African American and was convicted of numerous drug offenses over the years which led to multiple prison sentences.

He was drafted out of Oklahoma State, with a degree but illiterate, in the 1981 NFL Draft by the Washington Redskins in the fifth round with the one hundred nineteenth pick. He would play nine seasons for them, one for the Phoenix Cardinals, and one for the Tampa Bay Buccaneers appearing in one hundred forty three games before earning a lifetime ban from the NFL.

Dexter played defensive end and recorded ninety seven and a half sacks and two interceptions in his NFL career along with winning two Super Bowls in 1983 and 1988.

Dexter resurfaced in the Canadian Football League with the Ottawa Rough Riders playing in parts of two seasons with them appearing in five games.

Tommy Morrison was a former professional boxer who was convicted of numerous drug and firearm charges.

He was a heavyweight who appeared in fifty two fights compiling a 48-3-1 career record with forty two knockouts and would win the heavyweight world title in 1993 by defeating George Foreman. However he is probably more well known for his role as Tommy "The Machine" Gunn in the movie Rocky V and his battle with HIV.

Tommy died at the Nebraska Medical Center in Omaha on September 1st in 2013 at the age of forty four from cardiac arrest.

Eric Naposki is a former professional football player who was convicted of murder.

He went undrafted out of University of Connecticut in 1988 before being signed by the New England Patriots who he played parts of two seasons for appearing in four games. He would finish parts of the second season in the NFL with the Indianapolis Colts appearing in one game. In all he played in five games.

Eric played linebacker in his NFL career.

Eric resurfaced in the World League of American Football with the Barcelona Dragons playing four seasons for them while recording sixteen and a half sacks and one interception in his WLAF career along with winning the World Bowl in 1997.

Judith Neelley is a female serial killer who along with her husband and partner Alvin Neelley were convicted of two murders and one attempted murder. She experienced the death of her alcoholic father when she was only nine before eloping with a much older Alvin while she was underage.

At the time of the murders Judith was pregnant and would give birth behind bars.

Alvin died in prison on October 21st in 2005 at the age of fifty two from a surgical complication.

Dennis Nilsen was a serial killer from England who was convicted of six murders, one attempted murder, and also suspected in many other murders. He was a homosexual Army veteran with a history of drinking who was diagnosed narcissistic by multiple psychiatrists during his trial.

I would write Dennis twice as I really wanted to converse with him, but never got a response. Over the years I have seen very little if any of his letters being sold online. He was often referred to as the British Jeffrey Dahmer.

Dennis died in prison on May 12th in 2018 at the age of seventy two from a pulmonary embolism.

> "If you can't be a good example, at least be a horrible warning."
> Aileen Wuornos

XXXXVII.

James Parker who along with Robert Tulloch were convicted of two murders. James was sixteen and Robert was seventeen at the time of the murders.

Their crimes occurred in the neighboring state to me, New Hampshire. I hoped by writing James I may be able to visit him at some point. He would never answer however.

Evan Ramsey is a mass killer and school shooter who was convicted of two murders and two attempted murders at the Bethel Regional High School in Alaska.

As a young child Evan's father would be imprisoned for a standoff with the police while his mother was an alcoholic. This led to Evan entering the foster care world where he would be both physically and sexually abused and attempt suicide at the age of ten.

Once adopted he would be bullied in school. Years later the video game Doom would be brought up as a possible component to his crimes.

I think this is a great argument to make. The vast majority of the public will say video games don't create a killer.

Agreed, they can't create a killer, but I definitely believe they can be part of the creation process by influencing an already unstable mind.

We all have heard the saying, 'practice makes perfect'. You do something enough times you get good or at least better at it. Another way to look at it is, it becomes easier.

A damaged mind, which Evan's clearly was through his experiences alone, has therefore been practicing to kill. As a young adult your brain is still developing and it is also a time where mental health issues can manifest themselves and influence an individual's decision making and thought process.

Another example is a coroner or medical examiner when watching or helping out on their first autopsy during their early studies will be nauseous or even throw up, but after years and hundreds of autopsies, can eat their lunch while doing one. They are now desensitized, much like the young damaged mind becomes playing a violent video game over and over. The only difference is a stable mind can deal with it, and unstable mind can't deal with it properly.

I believe we need to take this more seriously and that starts with the parents who know their children better than anyone. They are the only line of defense anymore.

Years ago ratings on a movie or music album meant something and were enforced. Now, nobody cares. Video games carry them now to, but no stores enforce those either, none that I've seen anyway.

One of the biggest selling game series of all time is Grand Theft Auto which repeatedly has the player engage in sex with prostitutes, murder police officers and numerous racist actions for which you are rewarded.

Television is no different. Every show now has nudity, sex scenes, swearing, and violence. As I write this, Halloween just made seventy seven million at the box office. The movies with the most violence or sex, like Fifty Shades Of Grey, which I will come back to in a later chapter, make the most money. Some people will argue, but what about movies like Harry Potter or any of the new super hero movies. They are equally as important. They represent fantasy.

A harmless movie like Batman led an unstable man, James Holmes, to dress up as a character from the movie and murder twelve people and injury seventy others. So imagine what happens if he were to play Doom? Grand Theft Auto? If he saw Halloween instead, would he have become a serial killer rather than a mass killer as his character The Joker was.

I will continue with this in the conclusion section but the debate needed to be started here due to the game Doom and its role in the killings.

Next up for my rejections was Robert Rhoades.

Robert Rhoades, "The Truck Stop Killer", is a serial killer who was convicted of three murders but suspected of more than fifty. He was a former Marine whose father had been arrested for a sexual assault on a twelve year old girl. While awaiting trial on that charge the father would commit suicide. Over the Years Robert would be married three times.

Richard Rogers, "The Last Call Killer", is a serial killer who was convicted of two murders but suspected of numerous others. He was a homosexual nurse who surprisingly didn't kill at work but instead found his victims at gay bars.

Darlie Routier is a female killer who was convicted of murdering one of her three sons, even though she had killed two of them. The third was asleep upstairs with her husband.

She blamed a mysterious intruder for the crimes and alleged he attacked her as well but she survived with a slash on her throat.

She maintains her innocence even now and has a website set up about her case. On this site it was encouraged to write her and offer support. I did this and never received a response. I'm guessing because I didn't enclose a donation.

Susan Smith was a female killer convicted of the murders of her two children. Her crimes were famous as she blamed an imaginary suspect. This suspect had carjacked her car and kidnapped her two children setting off a manhunt and media frenzy. She would confess over a week later and lead police to the lake she drove the car into to drown them.

Her father had committed suicide when Susan was just six. She herself would then try to take her own life at thirteen. She also had been molested by her mother's new husband. During the trial Susan received a diagnosis of having a dependent personality disorder and another of suffering from major depression.

I read how she was putting ads up on prison dating websites so I found her ad and wrote her. She never answered and she pulled her ad shortly thereafter or the website pulled it after receiving bad publicity.

Cary Stayner, "The Yosemite Killer", is a serial killer who was convicted of four murders. As a child his younger brother Steven was kidnapped by Kenneth Parnell, a career child molester with a history of time spent in mental institutions. After seven years Steven and another victim would escape. This story led to a book and movie named I Know My First Name Is Steven.

Steven unfortunately died in a motorcycle accident a few years later. Kenneth died in prison on January 21st in 2008 at the age of seventy six from natural causes.

Cary was living with an uncle shortly after Steven's death that he would later disclose molested him as a child. This uncle would be murdered and not long after Cary would attempt suicide and get involved in drugs.

During his trial both obsessive-compulsive disorder and paraphilia would be used as a diagnosis.

Jeremy Strohmeyer was convicted of the murder of a seven year old girl at the Primadonna Resort and Casino in Primm, Nevada. Jeremy was only eighteen at the time of the murder.

He had been adopted and during his trial his defense team would let the jury know that his biological father was in prison and his biological mother was in a mental institution.

This case would bring about changes and new laws concerning children and their safety at casinos.

Marybeth Tinning is a female serial killer who was convicted of the murder of her ninth child but suspected of murdering the previous eight children as well.

She along with Darlie Routier and Susan Smith are very unique because they could be classified as a family annihilator, which we remember is defined as someone who kills at least two of their immediate family members often in a mass event. However, family annihilators tend to kill a spouse or other adult in the event, along with children. Darlie and Susan make a case to fit in this category because their murders were a single event and had at least two victims. Marybeth's was individual murders over years making her fall into the serial killer category.

Marybeth would claim physical abuse by her father while a child but was still convicted. After her conviction she would be rejected for parole six times before the New York parole board granted her a release on August 21st in 2018.

I would visit the graves of her children in 2012 and found it interesting that the children are buried in two different cemeteries. Barbara Ann Tinning, Jennifer Lewis Tinning, Jonathan Tinning, Joseph A. Tinning Jr., Mary Frances Tinning, Nathan Tinning, and Timothy M. Tinning are in Most Holy Redeemer Cemetery while Michael Raymond Tinning and Tami Lynne Tinning are in Schenectady Memorial Park. Both cemeteries are located in upstate New York.

Ward Weaver III was convicted of two murders. As mentioned before he is the son of a serial killer, Ward Weaver Jr., and the father of a killer, Francis Weaver.

While in prison he was attacked by another inmate with a shank on March 4th in 2007 but managed to survive.

Stanley "Tookie" Williams was African American and was convicted of four murders. He is known as one of the founders of the Crips, an African American gang and for being nominated for the Nobel Peace Prize while on death row. As a child his father abandoned the family.

Stanley was executed at San Quentin State Prison on December 13th in 2005 at the age of fifty one by lethal injection.

His last meal consisted of oatmeal and milk.

One of Stanley's sons would end up in prison for murder as well. Stanley "Little Tookie" Williams IV, also a Crip, would be given a sixteen year sentence for a shooting.

Wayne Williams is a serial killer who is African American and who was convicted of two murders but suspected of many more. Wayne has maintained his innocence over the years and there are many people who believe he may be innocent or not the killer of all the victims linked to him.

I wrote him wanting to discuss this and was surprised he never answered. Over the years I have not seen many of his letters being sold meaning he rarely answers strangers.

James Wood was a serial killer who was convicted of one murder but suspected of many more. During his early years he experienced his father being incarcerated at Leavenworth Penitentiary and his mother dying in a fire.

I wrote him after seeing some of his art, which I thought was very unique. He would paint on pieces of wood. In my opinion they were very good. Unfortunately he never answered my letter. He instead gave my contact information to fellow death row inmate James Hairston who I mentioned earlier.

James died in prison on February 1st in 2004 at the age of fifty six from a heart attack.

Aileen Wuornos was a female serial killer who was convicted of six murders. Her early life is filled with so much trauma it is not surprising what she became. She is the last killer I will talk about before I analyze the facts and go over my conclusions, and what better one then her, a great example of nature and nurture both going wrong.

Starting with the nature aspect Aileen's father was a schizophrenic who served prison time for sexually abusing children. While in prison he would commit suicide. Her grandfather, who would raise her, was an alcoholic.

As for the nurture side Aileen never met her father, was abandoned by her mother, molested by her grandfather, and raped by one of his friends.

Aileen would become a hardcore alcoholic who was considered a psychopath by many experts.

Aileen was executed on October 9th in 2002 at the age of forty six by lethal injection.

She declined a last meal. Her last words were: "Yes, I would just like to say I'm sailing with the rock, and I'll be back, like Independence Day, with Jesus. June 6, like the movie. Big mother ship and all, I'll be back, I'll be back."

I have discussed so many subjects up to this point. The following sections will break the data down for you before I give you my observations and conclusions.

Graves of Marybeth Tinning's children

RESEARCH TOTALS

CORRESPONDENCES (105)

ANDREWS, RALPH – 1
ANGELO, RICHARD – 1
BAR-JONAH, NATHANIEL – 5
BARDO, ROBERT – 4
BITTAKER, LAWRENCE – 19
BONIN, WILLIAM – 2
BOWLES, GARY – 16
BRADY, IAN – 5
BRIGHT, LARRY – 1
BROWN, ALFRED – 1
BRUDOS, JEROME – 4
CARIGNAN, HARVEY – 1
CHERRY, RAPHEL – 4
CLARK, DOUGLAS – 3
CLARK, HADDEN – 11
CONAHAN, DANIEL – 1
CONNER, DARION – 4
CORNELIUS, TINA – 6
CORNETT, NATASHA – 1
CORONA, JUAN – 1
CRAFTS, RICHARD – 1
CURTIS, CHAD – 1
DARDAR, RAMSEY – 2
DILLON, THOMAS – 9
DREW, CARL – 1
ETIENNE, CLIFFORD – 1
FARLEY, RICHARD – 2
FERGUSON, COLIN – 1
FRANCOIS, KENDALL – 24
GACY, JOHN – 3
GALLEGO, GERALD – 1
GAYNOR, ALFRED – 1
GECHT, ROBIN – 1
GORE, DAVID – 2
GRAHAM, DAVID – 1
GRAHAM, HARRISON – 4
GRAY, DANA – 3
GREINEDER, DIRK – 2
HEIRENS, WILLIAM – 35
HENLEY, DARRYL – 4
HENLEY, ELMER – 4
HILTON, DAVE JR. – 2
HOUSTON, ERIC – 9
JABLONSKI, PHILLIP – 1
JACKSON, CALVIN – 6
JESPERSON, KEITH – 2
JONES, BRYAN – 8
JONES, GENENE – 3
JONES, JEREMY – 1
JOYNER, ANTHONY – 2
KEARNEY, PATRICK – 3
KINKEL, KIP – 1
KRAFT, RANDY – 7
LO, WAYNE – 68
LONG, BOBBY – 2
LUCAS, HENRY – 2
MAIMONI, THOMAS – 61
MAJORS, ORVILLE – 1

MARQUETTE, RICHARD – 45
MAXWELL, BOBBY – 1
MCWATTERS, EUGENE – 1
MENDENHALL, BRUCE – 1
MULLIN, HERBERT – 1
MUNRO, JAMES – 1
NG, CHARLES – 3
NORRIS, ROY – 2
OLSON, CLIFFORD – 15
PARKER, GERALD – 1
PAYNE, THOMAS – 4
PETERSON, SCOTT – 2
PICKTON, ROBERT – 2
PIKE, CHRISTA – 4
PRINCE, CLEOPHUS – 8
RABBITT, DENNIS – 4
RAMIREZ, RICHARD – 39
RAY, CYNTHIA – 2
RIFKIN, JOEL – 1
RISSELL, MONTIE – 5
RIVA, JAMES – 1
RIZZO, TODD – 1
ROGERS, DAYTON – 2
ROGERS, GLEN – 1
ROSS, MICHAEL – 73
RUSSELL, GEORGE – 1
SALCIDO, RAMON – 3
SAMPSON, GARY – 4
SCHAEFER, GERALD – 1
SCHLICHTER, ART – 3
SEDA, HERIBERTO – 1
SELLS, TOMMY – 1
SHAWCROSS, ARTHUR – 16
SHERMANTINE, WESLEY – 1
SMART, PAMELA – 5
SMITH, ROBERT – 1
STANO, GERALD – 1
SUTCLIFFE, PETER – 4
TERRY, MICHAEL – 14
TRAWICK, JACK – 2
WALLACE, HENRY – 6
WARMUS, CAROLYN – 2
WEAVER, WARD JR. – 4
WEBB, EMANUEL – 2
WILSON, JOHN – 8
WOODFIELD, RANDALL – 20
YATES, ROBERT – 4

LETTERS – 697

TOTAL SUBJECTS (116)

ANDREWS, RALPH
ANGELO, RICHARD
BAR-JONAH, NATHANIEL
BARDO, ROBERT
BITTAKER, LAWRENCE
BIZANOWICZ, MICHAEL
BONIN, WILLIAM
BOWLES, GARY
BRADY, IAN
BRIGHT, LARRY
BROWN, ALFRED
BRUDOS, JEROME
CARIGNAN, HARVEY
CHERRY, RAPHEL
CLARK, DOUGLAS
CLARK, HADDEN
CONAHAN, DANIEL
CONNER, DARION
CORNELIUS, TINA
CORNETT, NATASHA
CORONA, JUAN
CRAFTS, RICHARD
CURTIS, CHAD
DARDAR, RAMSEY
DILLON, THOMAS
DREW, CARL
DRUCE, JOSEPH
ETIENNE, CLIFFORD
EVICCI, WILFRED
FARLEY, RICHARD
FERGUSON, COLIN
FRANCOIS, KENDALL
FULLER, JAMIE
GACY, JOHN
GALLEGO, GERALD
GAYNOR, ALFRED
GECHT, ROBIN
GORE, DAVID
GRAHAM, DAVID
GRAHAM, HARRISON
GRAY, DANA
GREINEDER, DIRK
HEIRENS, WILLIAM
HENLEY, DARRYL
HENLEY, ELMER
HILTON, DAVE JR.
HOUSTON, ERIC
JABLONSKI, PHILLIP
JACKSON, CALVIN
JESPERSON, KEITH
JONES, BRYAN
JONES, GENENE
JONES, JEREMY
JOYNER, ANTHONY
KEARNEY, PATRICK
KINKEL, KIP
KRAFT, RANDY
LEAHY, PAUL

LO, WAYNE
LONG, BOBBY
LUCAS, HENRY
MAIMONI, THOMAS
MAJORS, ORVILLE
MARQUETTE, RICHARD
MAXWELL, BOBBY
MCCOLLOM, EUGENE
MCCOWEN, CHRISTOPHER
MCDERMOTT, MICHAEL
MCWATTERS, EUGENE
MENDENHALL, BRUCE
MULLIN, HERBERT
MUNRO, JAMES
NASSAR, GEORGE
NG, CHARLES
NORRIS, ROY
OLSON, CLIFFORD
PARKER, GERALD
PAYNE, THOMAS
PETERSON, SCOTT
PICKTON, ROBERT
PIKE, CHRISTA
PRINCE, CLEOPHUS
RABBITT, DENNIS
RAMIREZ, RICHARD
RAY, CYNTHIA
RIFKIN, JOEL
RISSELL, MONTIE
RIVA, JAMES
RIZZO, TODD
ROGERS, DAYTON
ROGERS, GLEN
ROSS, MICHAEL
RUSSELL, GEORGE
SALCIDO, RAMON
SAMPSON, GARY
SCHAEFER, GERALD
SCHLICHTER, ART
SEDA, HERIBERTO
SELLS, TOMMY
SHAWCROSS, ARTHUR
SHERMANTINE, WESLEY
SMART, PAMELA
SMITH, ROBERT
SOSA, CHE
STANO, GERALD
SUTCLIFFE, PETER
TAVARES, DANIEL
TERRY, MICHAEL
TRAWICK, JACK
WALLACE, HENRY
WARMUS, CAROLYN
WEAVER, WARD JR.
WEBB, EMANUEL
WILSON, JOHN
WOODFIELD, RANDALL
YATES, ROBERT

CATEGORIES

HIGH PROFILE KILLERS (18/15.51%)

BARDO, ROBERT

BIZANOWICZ, MICHAEL

CORNELIUS, TINA

CRAFTS, RICHARD

DRUCE, JOSEPH

FULLER, JAMIE

GRAHAM, DAVID

GREINEDER, DIRK

LEAHY, PAUL

MAIMONI, THOMAS

MCCOWEN, CHRISTOPHER

PETERSON, SCOTT

PIKE, CHRISTA

RAY, CYNTHIA

RIVA, JAMES

RIZZO, TODD

SMART, PAMELA

WARMUS, CAROLYN

MASS KILLERS (8/6.89%)

BROWN, ALFRED

CORNETT, NATASHA

FARLEY, RICHARD

FERGUSON, COLIN

HOUSTON, ERIC

LO, WAYNE

MCDERMOTT, MICHAEL

SMITH, ROBERT

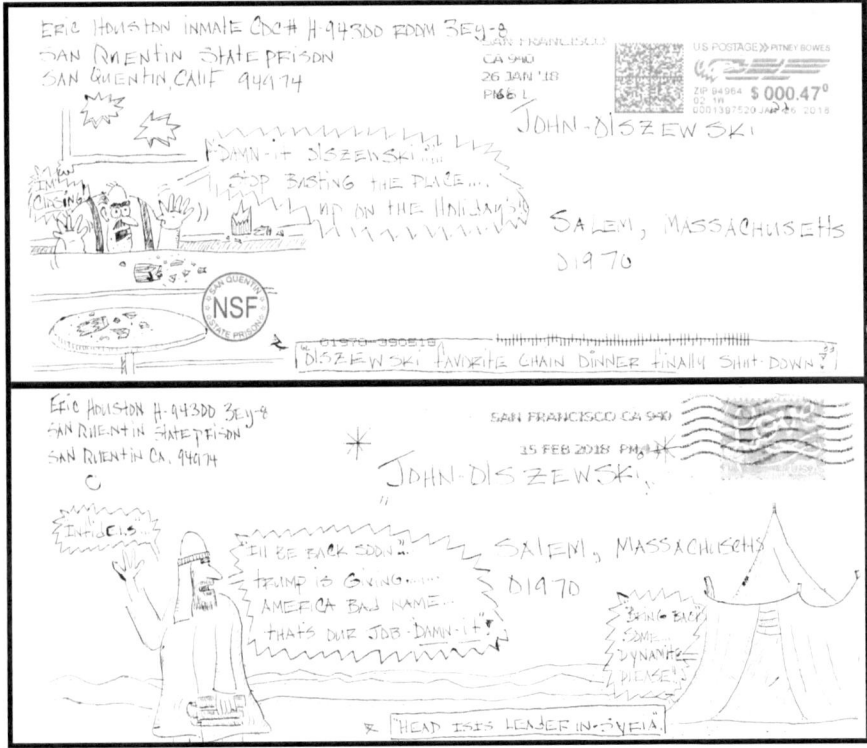

Envelopes from Eric Houston

PROFESSIONAL ATHLETES (10/8.62%)

CHERRRY, RAPHEL – FOOTBALL

CONNER, DARION – FOOTBALL

CURTIS, CHAD – BASEBALL

DARDAR, RAMSEY – FOOTBALL

ETIENNE, CLIFFORD – BOXING

HENLEY, DARRYL – FOOTBALL

HILTON, DAVE JR. – BOXING

PAYNE, THOMAS – BASKETBALL & BOXING

SCHLICHTER, ART – FOOTBALL

WILSON, JOHN – FOOTBALL

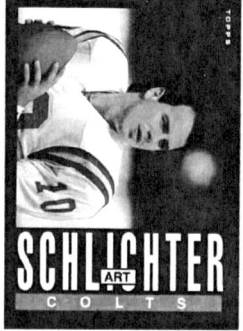

SERIAL KILLERS (74/63.79%)

ANDREWS, RALPH	MCCOLLOM, EUGENE
ANGELO, RICHARD	MCWATTERS, EUGENE
BAR-JONAH, NATHANIEL	MENDENHALL, BRUCE
BITTAKER, LAWRENCE	MULLIN, HERBERT
BONIN, WILLIAM	MUNRO, JAMES
BOWLES, GARY	NASSAR, GEORGE
BRADY, IAN	NG, CHARLES
BRIGHT, LARRY	NORRIS, ROY
BRUDOS, JEROME	OLSON, CLIFFORD
CARIGNAN, HARVEY	PARKER, GERALD
CLARK, DOUGLAS	PICKTON, ROBERT
CLARK, HADDEN	PRINCE, CLEOPHUS
CONAHAN, DANIEL	RAMIREZ, RICHARD
CORONA, JUAN	RIFKIN, JOEL
DILLON, THOMAS	RISSELL, MONTIE
DREW, CARL	ROGERS, DAYTON
FRANCOIS, KENDALL	ROGERS, GLEN
GACY, JOHN	ROSS, MICHAEL
GALLEGO, GERALD	RUSSELL, GEORGE
GAYNOR, ALFRED	SCHAEFER, GERALD
GECHT, ROBIN	SEDA, HERIBERTO
GORE, DAVID	SELLS, TOMMY
GRAHAM, HARRISON	SHAWCROSS, ARTHUR
GRAY, DANA	SHERMANTINE, WESLEY
HEIRENS, WILLIAM	STANO, GERALD
HENLEY, ELMER	SUTCLIFFE, PETER
JABLONSKI, PHILLIP	TAVARES, DANIEL
JACKSON, CALVIN	TERRY, MICHAEL
JESPERSON, KEITH	TRAWICK, JACK
JONES, BRYAN	WALLACE, HENRY
JONES, GENENE	WEAVER, WARD JR.
JONES, JEREMY	WEBB, EMANUEL
JOYNER, ANTHONY	WOODFIELD, RANDALL
KEARNEY, PATRICK	YATES, ROBERT
KRAFT, RANDY	
LONG, BOBBY	
LUCAS, HENRY	
MAJORS, ORVILLE	
MARQUETTE, RICHARD	
MAXWELL, BOBBY	

SERIAL RAPISTS (4/3.44%)

EVICCI, WILFRED

PAYNE, THOMAS

RABBITT, DENNIS

SOSA, CHE

Thomas Payne

SPREE KILLERS (3/2.58%)

KINKEL, KIP

SALCIDO, RAMON

SAMPSON, GARY

Gary Sampson

SUBCATEGORIES

ANGELS OF DEATH (3)

ANGELO, RICHARD

JONES, GENENE

MAJORS, ORVILLE

Genene Jones

CANNIBALS (4)

BAR-JONAH, NATHANIEL

CLARK, HADDEN

PICKTON, ROBERT

SHAWCROSS, ARTHUR

Mr Nathanael Bar-Jonah
AO 31569 MSP
700 Conley Lake Rd
Deer Lodge MT 59722

Jalapeño-Stuffed Pork Tenderloin

Prep: 30 min.   Marinating: 8 hr.   Grilling: 30 min.   Standing: 10 min.

1   1- to 1¼-lb. pork tenderloin
6   fresh jalapeño peppers, seeded and chopped
1   roma tomato, chopped
2   Tbsp. snipped fresh cilantro
2   Tbsp. lime juice
5   cloves garlic, minced
¼   cup butter or margarine

Trim fat from meat. Starting at center, cut a horizontal slit to the right and one to the left. Spread open. Cover with plastic wrap. Working from center, pound with flat side of mallet to ½-inch thickness. Remove wrap.

In bowl, combine *half* of the jalapeño peppers, tomato, cilantro, lime juice, garlic, and ¼ teaspoon *salt*. Sprinkle onto meat. Starting from a long side, roll up into a spiral, tucking in ends. Tie at 1-inch intervals with 100-percent-cotton string; place in a shallow dish. Cover; marinate in refrigerator 8 to 24 hours.

At serving time, melt butter; stir in remaining jalapeño peppers and ¼ teaspoon *salt*.

For a charcoal grill, arrange medium-hot coals around a drip pan. Test for medium heat above pan. Place meat on grill rack over drip pan. Cover and grill for 30 to 45 minutes or until meat is slightly pink near center and juices run clear, brushing occasionally with butter mixture the first 20 minutes of grilling. (For a gas grill, preheat grill. Reduce heat to medium. Adjust for indirect cooking. Grill as above, except place meat on a rack in a pan.)

Discard remaining butter mixture. Remove meat. Cover with foil; let stand for 10 minutes. Remove string; slice meat. Season with *black pepper* and additional *salt*. Serves 4 to 6.

Per serving: 260 cal., 16 g total fat (9 g sat. fat), 106 mg chol., 543 mg sodium, 4 g carbo., 1 g fiber, 25 g pro. Dietary exchanges: 0.5 vegetable, 3.5 very lean meat, 3 fat.

One of serial killer Nathaniel Bar-Jonah's favorite recipes

CULT KILLERS (3)

CORNETT, NATASHA

DREW, CARL

GECHT, ROBIN

Harper Collins, 1991

FAMILY ANNIHILATORS (5)

BROWN, ALFRED

CORNETT, NATASHA

KINKEL, KIP

PETERSON, SCOTT

SALCIDO, RAMON

Lavender Cookies
One of Laci's favorite Recipes

5/8 c   butter
½ c   white sugar
1   egg
1 T   lavender flowers
1 ½ c   all purpose flour
optional for decorating:
½ c   colored sugar
1 T   lavender flowers

1) Preheat oven to 350 degrees
2) Cream together the butter and sugar. Beat the egg, and blend into the butter and sugar. Mix in the lavender flowers and the flour. Drop batter by teaspoonfuls onto cookie sheets.
3) Bake 15-20 minutes, or until golden. Remove cookies to cooling racks, and sprinkle with decorative sugar and additional lavender flowers if desired.

Lacy Peterson's favorite recipe sent by Scott Peterson's mother who often responded on his behalf.

SCHOOL SHOOTERS (3)

HOUSTON, ERIC

KINKEL, KIP

LO, WAYNE

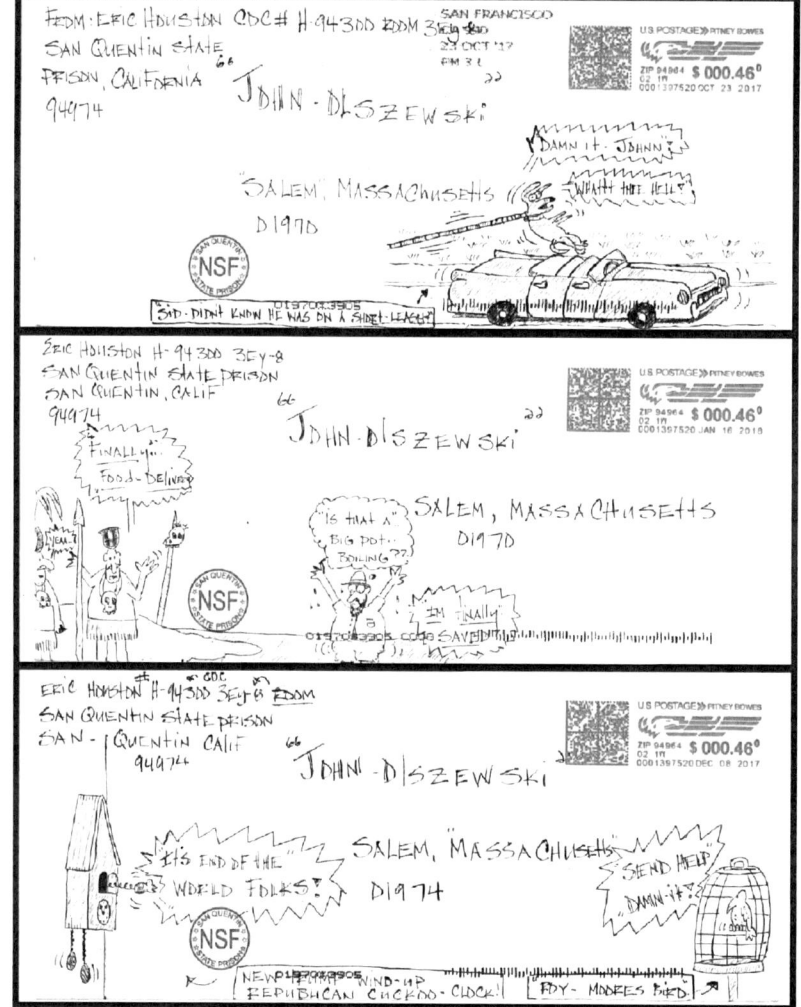

Envelopes from Eric Houston

TEAM KILLERS (12)

BITTAKER, LAWRENCE

BONIN, WILLIAM

BRADY, IAN

CLARK, DOUGLAS

GALLEGO, GERALD

GORE, DAVID

GRAHAM, DAVID

HENLEY, ELMER

MUNRO, JAMES

NG, CHARLES

NORRIS, ROY

SHERMANTINE, WESLEY

Origami made by Charles Ng

TEEN KILLERS (10)

BROWN, ALFRED

CORNETT, NATASHA

FULLER, JAMIE

HENLEY, ELMER

KINKEL, KIP

LO, WAYNE

PIKE, CHRISTA

RISSELL, MONTIE

RIZZO, TODD

SMITH, ROBERT

Wayne Lo

WORKPLACE SHOOTERS (2)

FARLEY, RICHARD

MCDERMOTT, MICHAEL

Christmas card from Richard Farley

BACKGROUNDS

FAMILY HISTORY/GENETIC INDICATORS (26/22.41%)

BITTAKER, LAWRENCE – Adopted.

BONIN, WILLIAM – Alcoholic father died when he was fourteen. Grandfather was a convicted child molester.

BOWLES, GARY – Father died six months before he was born.

CLARK, DOUGLAS – Family moved around constantly, making it hard to form friendships.

CLARK, HADDEN – Brother was convicted of strangling a woman. Alcoholic father committed suicide.

GACY, JOHN – Father was an alcoholic and nephew was convicted of sexual assault.

GALLEGO, GERALD – Father was executed for killing a police officer. Mother was a prostitute.

GRAY, DANA – Parents divorced when she was two.

HENLEY, ELMER – Father was an alcoholic.

JACKSON, CALVIN – Grandmother spent time in a mental hospital. Uncle was a child molester.

JONES, GENENE – Adopted.

LONG, BOBBY – Cousin of serial killer Henry Lucas.

LUCAS, HENRY – Cousin of serial killer Bobby Long. Father died when he was thirteen. Mother was a prostitute.

MCCOLLOM, EUGENE – Younger brother was murdered.

PIKE, CHRISTA – Mother was an alcoholic.

PRINCE, CLEOPHUS – Father was convicted of killing a man. Uncle was convicted of killing his wife.

RABBITT, DENNIS – Mother was murdered by his stepfather.

RIFKIN, JOEL – Adopted.

RISSELL, MONTE – Father left the family when he was only seven.

ROSS, MICHAEL – Uncle committed suicide.

SELLS, TOMMY – Twin sister died when he was around two.

SHERMANTINE, WESLEY – Mother was an alcoholic.

SMITH, ROBERT – Family moved around constantly, making it hard to form friendships.

STANO, GERALD – Adopted.

WARMUS, CAROLYN – Parents divorced when she was eight.

WEAVER, WARD JR. – Son was convicted of killing two girls.

HOMOSEXUAL TENDENCIES (12/10.34%)

BAR-JONAH, NATHANIEL

BONIN, WILLIAM

BOWLES, GARY

CONAHAN, DANIEL

CORONA, JUAN

GACY, JOHN

HENLEY, ELMER

KEARNEY, PATRICK

KRAFT, RANDY

MAJORS, ORVILLE

MUNRO, JAMES

TERRY, MICHAEL

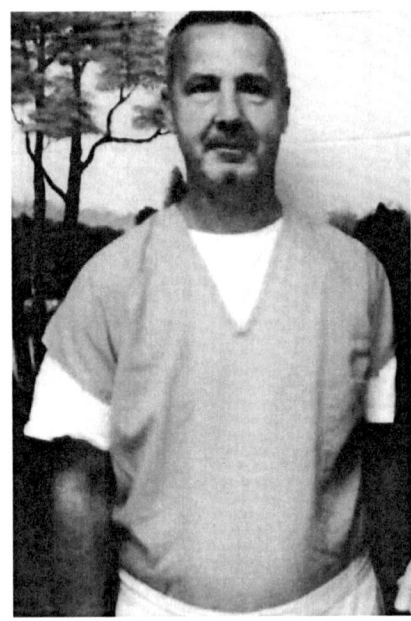

Gary Ray Bowles

MACDONALD TRIAD INDICATORS (7/6.03%)

BRADY, IAN – Cruelty To Animals

CARIGNAN, HARVEY – Bedwetting

CLARK, HADDEN – Cruelty To Animals

JESPERSON, KEITH – Cruelty To Animals

SCHAEFER, GERALD – Cruelty To Animals

SHAWCROSS, ARTHUR – Bedwetting & Fire Setting

STANO, GERALD – Bedwetting

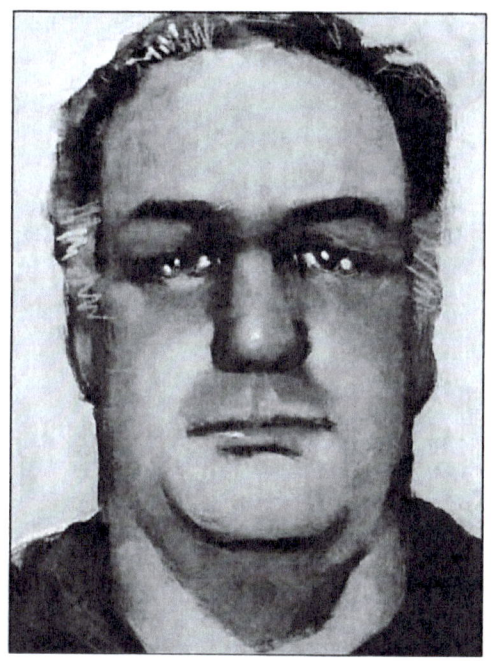

ARTHUR SHAWCROSS

MEDICAL ISSUES (17/14.65%)

BRUDOS, JEROME – Liver Cancer

CARIGNAN, HARVEY – Chorea

CORONA, JUAN – Dementia

DARDAR, RAMSEY – Borderline Intellectual Functioning

FRANCOIS, KENDALL – HIV

GACY, JOHN – Seizures

HEIRENS, WILLIAM – Diabetes

KINKEL, KIP – Dyslexia

LONG, BOBBY – Head Injuries & XXY Syndrome

LUCAS, HENRY – Lost an eye due to infection.

RAMIREZ, RICHARD – B-Cell Lymphoma, Head Injuries & Hepatitis C

RIFKIN, JOEL – Dyslexia

ROGERS, GLEN – Borderline Intellectual Functioning

SAMPSON, GARY – Head Injuries

SCHLICHTER, ART – Dementia, Head Injuries & Parkinson's Disease

SELLS, TOMMY – Borderline Intellectual Functioning & Meningitis

SHAWCROSS, ARTHUR – Head Injuries & XYY Syndrome

MENTAL HEALTH ISSUES (30/25.86%)

ANGELO, RICARD – Dissociative Identity Disorder

BARDO, ROBERT – Manic Depression

BITTAKER, LAWRENCE – Antisocial Personality

BRADY, IAN – Antisocial Personality

BRUDOS, JEROME – Necrophilia & Schizophrenia

CLARK, DOUGLAS – Necrophilia

CLARK, HADDEN – Paranoid Schizophrenia

CORNETT, NATASHA – Bipolar

CORONA, JUAN – Schizophrenia

FERGUSON, COLIN – Paranoid Schizophrenia

GACY, JOHN – Antisocial Personality

GRAHAM, HARRISON – Dissociative Identity Disorder

JESPERSON, KEITH – Suicide Attempts

KINKEL, KIP – Depression & Paranoid Schizophrenia

LO, WAYNE – Narcissistic Personality

LUCAS, HENRY – Antisocial Personality & Necrophilia

MCDERMOTT, MICHAEL – Schizophrenia

MULLIN, HERBERT – Paranoid Schizophrenia

NASSAR, GEORGE – Schizophrenia

NG, CHARLES – Dependent Personality Disorder

NORRIS, ROY – Suicide Attempt

RAY, CYNTHIA – Bipolar

RIVA, JAMES – Spent time in a mental hospital

ROSS, MICHAEL – Antisocial Personality

SAMPSON, GARY – Antisocial Personality

SELLS, TOMMY – Bipolar

SHAWCROSS, ARTHUR – Antisocial Personality & Necrophilia

SUTCLIFFE, PETER – Paranoid Schizophrenia

WOODFIELD, RANDALL – Antisocial Personality

YATES, ROBERT – Necrophilia

MILITARY SERVICE (19/16.37%)

BONIN, WILLIAM – AIR FORCE

CARIGNAN, HARVEY – ARMY

CLARK, DOUGLAS – AIR FORCE

CLARK, HADDEN – NAVY

CONAHAN, DANIEL – NAVY

FARLEY, RICHARD – NAVY

FRANCOIS, KENDALL – ARMY

GRAHAM, DAVID – AIR FORCE

JABLONSKI, PHILLIP – ARMY

KRAFT, RANDY – AIR FORCE

MCDERMOTT, MICHAEL – NAVY

NG, CHARLES – MARINES

NORRIS, ROY – NAVY

PARKER, GERALD – MARINES

PRINCE, CLEOPHUS – NAVY

RIZZO, TODD – MARINES

SHAWCROSS, ARTHUR – ARMY

WALLACE, HENRY – NAVY

YATES, ROBERT – ARMY

PAROLED TO KILL AGAIN (7/6.03%)

CARIGNAN, HARVEY

JABLONSKI, PHILLIP

LUCAS, HENRY

MARQUETTE, RICHARD

NASSAR, GEORGE

SHAWCROSS, ARTHUR

TAVARES, DANIEL

Serial killer Richard Marquette

PHYSICALLY ABUSED (17/14.65%)

BONIN, WILLIAM

BOWLES, GARY

BRUDOS, JEROME

CLARK, HADDEN

GACY, JOHN

HENLEY, ELMER

JACKSON, CALVIN

JESPERSON, KEITH

KEARNEY, PATRICK

LUCAS, HENRY

NG, CHARLES

PIKE, CHRISTA

RAMIREZ, RICHARD

RAY, CYNTHIA

ROSS, MICHAEL

SAMPSON, GARY

SHERMANTINE, WESLEY

SEXUALLY ABUSED (10/8.62%)

BONIN, WILLIAM

GACY, JOHN

JABLONSKI, PHILLIP

JESPERSON, KEITH

NORRIS, ROY

PIKE, CHRISTA

RAY, CYNTHIA

ROSS, MICHAEL

SELLS, TOMMY

SHAWCROSS, ARTHUR

SUBSTANCE ABUSERS (16/13.79%)

BRIGHT, LARRY

CONNER, DARION

CORNETT, NATASHA

ETIENNE, CLIFFORD

FULLER, JAMIE

GACY, JOHN

GAYNOR, ALFRED

GRAHAM, HARRISON

HENLEY, ELMER

MCWATTERS, EUGENE

MULLIN, HERBERT

NORRIS, ROY

RAMIREZ, RICHARD

SELLS, TOMMY

SHERMANTINE, WESLEY

WALLACE, HENRY

ETHNICITY

AFRICAN AMERICAN (23/19.82%)

CHERRY, RAPHEL

CONNER, DARION

DARDAR, RAMSEY

ETIENNE, CLIFFORD

FERGUSON, COLIN

FRANCOIS, KENDALL

GAYNOR, ALFRED

GRAHAM, HARRISON

HENLEY, DARRYL

JACKSON, CALVIN

JONES, BRYAN

JOYNER, ANTHONY

MAXWELL, BOBBY

MCCOWEN, CHRISTOPHER

PARKER, GERALD

PAYNE, THOMAS

PRINCE, CLEOPHUS

RUSSELL, GEORGE

SOSA, CHE

TERRY, MICHAEL

WALLACE, HENRY

WEBB, EMANUEL

WILSON, JOHN

ASIAN (3/2.58%)

BROWN, ALFRED

LO, WAYNE

NG, CHARLES

Wayne Lo

CAUCASIAN (86/74.13%)

ANDREWS, RALPH
ANGELO, RICHARD
BAR-JONAH, NATHANIEL
BARDO, ROBERT
BITTAKER, LAWRENCE
BIZANOWICZ, MICHAEL
BONIN, WILLIAM
BOWLES, GARY
BRADY, IAN
BRIGHT, LARRY
BRUDOS, JEROME
CARIGNAN, HARVEY
CLARK, DOUGLAS
CLARK, HADDEN
CONAHAN, DANIEL
CORNELIUS, TINA
CORNETT, NATASHA
CRAFTS, RICHARD
CURTIS, CHAD
DILLON, THOMAS
DREW, CARL
DRUCE, JOSEPH
EVICCI, WILFRED
FARLEY, RICHARD
FULLER, JAMIE
GACY, JOHN
GALLEGO, GERALD
GECHT, ROBIN
GORE, DAVID
GRAHAM, DAVID
GRAY, DANA
GREINEDER, DIRK
HEIRENS, WILLIAM
HENLEY, ELMER
HILTON, DAVE JR.
HOUSTON, ERIC
JABLONSKI, PHILLIP
JESPERSON, KEITH
JONES, GENENE
JONES, JEREMY
KEARNEY, PATRICK
KINKEL, KIP
KRAFT, RANDY
LEAHY, PAUL
LONG, BOBBY
LUCAS, HENRY
MAIMONI, THOMAS
MAJORS, ORVILLE
MARQUETTE, RICHARD
MCCOLLOM, EUGENE
MCDERMOTT, MICHAEL
MCWATTERS, EUGENE
MENDENHALL, BRUCE
MULLIN, HERBERT
MUNRO, JAMES
NASSAR, GEORGE
NORRIS, ROY
OLSON, CLIFFORD
PETERSON, SCOTT
PICKTON, ROBERT
PIKE, CHRISTA
RABBITT, DENNIS
RAY, CYNTHIA
RIFKIN, JOEL
RISSELL, MONTIE
RIVA, JAMES
RIZZO, TODD
ROGERS, DAYTON
ROGERS, GLEN
ROSS, MICHAEL
SAMPSON, GARY
SCHAEFER, GERALD
SCHLICHTER, ART
SELLS, TOMMY
SHAWCROSS, ARTHUR
SHERMANTINE, WESLEY
SMART, PAMELA
SMITH, ROBERT
STANO, GERALD
SUTCLIFFE, PETER
TAVARES, DANIEL
TRAWICK, JACK
WARMUS, CAROLYN
WEAVER, WARD JR.
WOODFIELD, RANDALL
YATES, ROBERT

LATINO (4/3.44%)

CORONA, JUAN

RAMIREZ, RICHARD

SALCIDO, RAMON

SEDA, HERIBERTO

RICHARD RAMIREZ

GENDER

FEMALES (8/6.89%)

CORNELIUS, TINA

CORNETT, NATASHA

GRAY, DANA

JONES, GENENE

PIKE, CHRISTA

RAY, CYNTHIA

SMART, PAMELA

WARMUS, CAROLYN

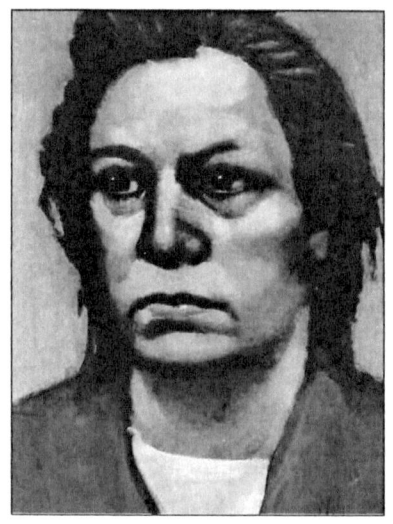

AILEEN WUORNOS

MALES (108/93.10%)

ANDREWS, RALPH
ANGELO, RICHARD
BAR-JONAH, NATHANIEL
BARDO, ROBERT
BITTAKER, LAWRENCE
BIZANOWICZ, MICHAEL
BONIN, WILLIAM
BOWLES, GARY
BRADY, IAN
BRIGHT, LARRY
BROWN, ALFRED
BRUDOS, JEROME
CARIGNAN, HARVEY
CHERRY, RAPHEL
CLARK, DOUGLAS
CLARK, HADDEN
CONAHAN, DANIEL
CONNER, DARION
CORONA, JUAN
CRAFTS, RICHARD
CURTIS, CHAD
DARDAR, RAMSEY
DILLON, THOMAS
DREW, CARL
DRUCE, JOSEPH
ETIENNE, CLIFFORD
EVICCI, WILFRED
FARLEY, RICHARD
FERGUSON, COLIN
FRANCOIS, KENDALL
FULLER, JAMIE
GACY, JOHN
GALLEGO, GERALD
GAYNOR, ALFRED
GECHT, ROBIN
GORE, DAVID
GRAHAM, DAVID
GRAHAM, HARRISON
GREINEDER, DIRK
HEIRENS, WILLIAM
HENLEY, DARRYL
HENLEY, ELMER
HILTON, DAVE JR.
HOUSTON, ERIC
JABLONSKI, PHILLIP
JACKSON, CALVIN
JESPERSON, KEITH
JONES, BRYAN
JONES, JEREMY
JOYNER, ANTHONY
KEARNEY, PATRICK
KINKEL, KIP
KRAFT, RANDY
LEAHY, PAUL

LO, WAYNE
LONG, BOBBY
LUCAS, HENRY
MAIMONI, THOMAS
MAJORS, ORVILLE
MARQUETTE, RICHARD
MAXWELL, BOBBY
MCCOLLOM, EUGENE
MCCOWEN, CHRISTOPHER
MCDERMOTT, MICHAEL
MCWATTERS, EUGENE
MENDENHALL, BRUCE
MULLIN, HERBERT
MUNRO, JAMES
NASSAR, GEORGE
NG, CHARLES
NORRIS, ROY
OLSON, CLIFFORD
PARKER, GERALD
PAYNE, THOMAS
PETERSON, SCOTT
PICKTON, ROBERT
PRINCE, CLEOPHUS
RABBITT, DENNIS
RAMIREZ, RICHARD
RIFKIN, JOEL
RISSELL, MONTIE
RIVA, JAMES
RIZZO, TODD
ROGERS, DAYTON
ROGERS, GLEN
ROSS, MICHAEL
RUSSELL, GEORGE
SALCIDO, RAMON
SAMPSON, GARY
SCHAEFER, GERALD
SCHLICHTER, ART
SEDA, HERIBERTO
SELLS, TOMMY
SHAWCROSS, ARTHUR
SHERMANTINE, WESLEY
SMITH, ROBERT
SOSA, CHE
STANO, GERALD
SUTCLIFFE, PETER
TAVARES, DANIEL
TERRY, MICHAEL
TRAWICK, JACK
WALLACE, HENRY
WEAVER, WARD JR.
WEBB, EMANUEL
WILSON, JOHN
WOODFIELD, RANDALL
YATES, ROBERT

GEOGRAPHY

AMERICAN (111/95.68%)

ANDREWS, RALPH
ANGELO, RICHARD
BAR-JONAH, NATHANIEL
BARDO, ROBERT
BITTAKER, LAWRENCE
BIZANOWICZ, MICHAEL
BONIN, WILLIAM
BOWLES, GARY
BRIGHT, LARRY
BROWN, ALFRED
BRUDOS, JEROME
CARIGNAN, HARVEY
CHERRY, RAPHEL
CLARK, DOUGLAS
CLARK, HADDEN
CONAHAN, DANIEL
CONNER, DARION
CORNELIUS, TINA
CORNETT, NATASHA
CORONA, JUAN
CRAFTS, RICHARD
CURTIS, CHAD
DARDAR, RAMSEY
DILLON, THOMAS
DREW, CARL
DRUCE, JOSEPH
ETIENNE, CLIFFORD
EVICCI, WILFRED
FARLEY, RICHARD
FERGUSON, COLIN
FRANCOIS, KENDALL
FULLER, JAMIE
GACY, JOHN
GALLEGO, GERALD
GAYNOR, ALFRED
GECHT, ROBIN
GORE, DAVID
GRAHAM, DAVID
GRAHAM, HARRISON
GRAY, DANA
GREINEDER, DIRK
HEIRENS, WILLIAM
HENLEY, DARRYL
HENLEY, ELMER
HOUSTON, ERIC
JABLONSKI, PHILLIP
JACKSON, CALVIN
JESPERSON, KEITH
JONES, BRYAN
JONES, GENENE
JONES, JEREMY
JOYNER, ANTHONY
KEARNEY, PATRICK
KINKEL, KIP
KRAFT, RANDY
LEAHY, PAUL
LO, WAYNE
LONG, BOBBY
LUCAS, HENRY
MAIMONI, THOMAS
MAJORS, ORVILLE
MARQUETTE, RICHARD
MAXWELL, BOBBY
MCCOLLOM, EUGENE
MCCOWEN, CHRISTOPHER
MCDERMOTT, MICHAEL
MCWATTERS, EUGENE
MENDENHALL, BRUCE
MULLIN, HERBERT
MUNRO, JAMES
NASSAR, GEORGE
NG, CHARLES
NORRIS, ROY
PARKER, GERALD
PAYNE, THOMAS
PETERSON, SCOTT
PIKE, CHRISTA
PRINCE, CLEOPHUS
RABBITT, DENNIS
RAMIREZ, RICHARD
RAY, CYNTHIA
RIFKIN, JOEL
RISSELL, MONTIE
RIVA, JAMES
RIZZO, TODD
ROGERS, DAYTON
ROGERS, GLEN
ROSS, MICHAEL
RUSSELL, GEORGE
SALCIDO, RAMON
SAMPSON, GARY
SCHAEFER, GERALD
SCHLICHTER, ART
SEDA, HERIBERTO
SELLS, TOMMY
SHAWCROSS, ARTHUR
SHERMANTINE, WESLEY
SMART, PAMELA
SMITH, ROBERT
SOSA, CHE
STANO, GERALD
TAVARES, DANIEL
TERRY, MICHAEL
TRAWICK, JACK
WALLACE, HENRY
WARMUS, CAROLYN
WEAVER, WARD JR.
WEBB, EMANUEL
WILSON, JOHN
WOODFIELD, RANDALL
YATES, ROBERT

FOREIGN (5/4.31%)

BRADY, IAN (ENGLAND)

HILTON, DAVE JR. (CANADA)

OLSON, CLIFFORD (CANADA)

PICKTON, ROBERT (CANADA)

SUTCLIFFE, PETER (ENGLAND)

Former professional boxer Dave Hilton Jr.

LOCAL (MASSACHUSETTS) (18/15.51%)

BIZANOWICZ, MICHAEL

BROWN, ALFRED

DREW, CARL

DRUCE, JOSEPH

EVICCI, WILFRED

FULLER, JAMIE

GAYNOR, ALFRED

GREINEDER, DIRK

LEAHY, PAUL

LO, WAYNE

MAIMONI, THOMAS

MCCOLLOM, EUGENE

MCCOWEN, CHRISTOPHER

MCDERMOTT, MICHAEL

NASSAR, GEORGE

RIVA, JAMES

SOSA, CHE

TAVARES, DANIEL

Grave of Albert DeSalvo

STATUS

ALIVE (91/78.44%)

ANGELO, RICHARD
BARDO, ROBERT
BITTAKER, LAWRENCE
BIZANOWICZ, MICHAEL
BOWLES, GARY
BRIGHT, LARRY
BROWN, ALFRED
CARIGNAN, HARVEY
CHERRY, RAPHEL
CLARK, DOUGLAS
CLARK, HADDEN
CONAHAN, DANIEL
CONNER, DARION
CORNELIUS, TINA
CORNETT, NATASHA
CRAFTS, RICHARD
CURTIS, CHAD
DARDAR, RAMSEY
DREW, CARL
DRUCE, JOSEPH
ETIENNE, CLIFFORD
EVICCI, WILFRED
FARLEY, RICHARD
FERGUSON, COLIN
FULLER, JAMIE
GAYNOR, ALFRED
GECHT, ROBIN
GRAHAM, DAVID
GRAHAM, HARRISON
GRAY, DANA
GREINEDER, DIRK
HENLEY, DARRYL
HENLEY, ELMER
HILTON, DAVE JR.
HOUSTON, ERIC
JABLONSKI, PHILLIP
JACKSON, CALVIN
JESPERSON, KEITH
JONES, BRYAN
JONES, GENENE
JONES, JEREMY
JOYNER, ANTHONY
KEARNEY, PATRICK
KINKEL, KIP
KRAFT, RANDY
LEAHY, PAUL
LO, WAYNE
MARQUETTE, RICHARD
MCCOLLOM, EUGENE
MCCOWEN, CHRISTOPHER
MCDERMOTT, MICHAEL
MCWATTERS, EUGENE
MENDENHALL, BRUCE
MULLIN, HERBERT
MUNRO, JAMES
NASSAR, GEORGE
NG, CHARLES
NORRIS, ROY
PARKER, GERALD
PAYNE, THOMAS
PETERSON, SCOTT
PICKTON, ROBERT
PIKE, CHRISTA
PRINCE, CLEOPHUS
RABBITT, DENNIS
RAY, CYNTHIA
RIFKIN, JOEL
RISSELL, MONTIE
RIVA, JAMES
RIZZO, TODD
ROGERS, DAYTON
ROGERS, GLEN
RUSSELL, GEORGE
SALCIDO, RAMON
SAMPSON, GARY
SCHLICHTER, ART
SEDA, HERIBERTO
SHERMANTINE, WESLEY
SMART, PAMELA
SMITH, ROBERT
SOSA, CHE
SUTCLIFFE, PETER
TAVARES, DANIEL
TERRY, MICHAEL
WALLACE, HENRY
WARMUS, CAROLYN
WEAVER, WARD JR.
WEBB, EMANUEL
WILSON, JOHN
WOODFIELD, RANDALL
YATES, ROBERT

DECEASED (25/21.55%)

EXECUTED (8/6.89%) **MURDERED (1/0.86%)** **NATURAL CAUSES (16/13.79%)**

ANDREWS, RALPH – Natural Causes in 2006.

BAR-JONAH, NATHANIEL – Natural Causes in 2008.

BONIN, WILLIAM – Executed in 1996.

BRADY, IAN – Natural Causes in 2017.

BRUDOS, JEROME – Natural Causes in 2006.

CORONA, JUAN – Natural Causes in 2019.

DILLON, THOMAS – Natural Causes in 2011.

FRANCOIS, KENDALL – Natural Causes in 2014.

GACY, JOHN – Executed in 1994.

GALLEGO, GERALD – Natural Causes in 2002.

GORE, DAVID – Executed in 2012.

HEIRENS, WILLIAM – Natural Causes in 2012.

LONG, BOBBY – Executed in 2019.

LUCAS, HENRY – Natural Causes in 2001.

MAIMONI, THOMAS – Natural Causes in 2017.

MAJORS, ORVILLE – Natural Causes in 2017.

MAXWELL, BOBBY – Natural Causes in 2019.

OLSON, CLIFFORD – Natural Causes in 2011.

RAMIREZ, RICHARD – Natural Causes in 2013.

ROSS, MICHAEL – Executed in 2005.

SCHAEFER, GERALD – Murdered in 1995.

SELLS, TOMMY – Executed in 2014.

SHAWCROSS, ARTHUR – Natural Causes in 2008.

STANO, GERALD – Executed in 1998.

TRAWICK, JACK – Executed in 2009.

> "I always had a desire to inflict pain on others and to have others inflict pain on me. I always seemed to enjoy everything that hurt."
>
> Albert Fish

XXXXVIII.

It has taken me a year and a half to get to this section of my book. Throughout that time I have constantly thought about what I would write and at times it has given me sleepless nights. There are so many things I want to say, yet I fear some of them may be taken the wrong way, or offend others. Ultimately this is the most important section of the book, the one that will be judged by those who read it.

This is where I make my observations and the reason I wanted my research totals put in print in the preceding pages. The most important of those pages were those that fell under the background section. I tried to come up with every possible circumstance that could contribute to the evolution of a killer.

By figuring out the percentages it shows just how common each trait is. When I explain each I will further break things down by eliminating the high profile killers, professional athletes and the serial rapists from the percentages in another effort to show how common each is specifically with the multiple murderers.

The first of the background factors was the family history and genetic indicators. I wanted to include such things among the subject's family as addiction, adoption, death, and also mention family members who had a criminal past or mental health issues.

We all know that I will never obtain all the data as some subjects and their families will never acknowledge certain things. For this first background factor I found twenty six or twenty two point four one percent of my one hundred sixteen subjects had family history and genetic indicators. After removing the high profile killers, professional athletes, and serial rapists, the total subjects is eighty five, my count drops to twenty three, but the percentage climbs to twenty seven point zero five percent, an increase of four point six four percent.

This means that more than one of every four multiple murderers have a family history or genetic indicator. That is an alarming start.

The second of the background factors is homosexual tendencies. This is not meant to imply homosexuality is something negative or a cause of why people commit multiple murders, but certain individuals may be raised in homes where it is frowned on or even forbidden. This can cause psychological damage to someone who now must hide this and bare shame. This can lead to a substance abuse problem to cope, further damaging this individual.

For this background factor I found twelve or ten point three four percent of my one hundred sixteen subjects had homosexual tendencies. After removing the high profile killers, professional athletes, and serial rapists, the total subjects is eighty five, my count stays at twelve, but the percentage climbs to fourteen point one one percent, an increase of three point seven seven percent.

Not as high at the family history and genetic indicators, but again a higher amount then the non-multiple murderers.

The third of the background factors is the MacDonald triad indicators. For this background factor I found seven or six point zero three percent of my one hundred sixteen subjects had MacDonald triad indicators. After removing the high profile killers, professional athletes, and serial rapists, the total subjects is eighty five, my count stays at seven, but the percentage climbs to eight point two three percent, an increase of two point two zero percent.

That makes three for three with higher results for the multiple murderers.

The fourth of the background factors is medical issues. For this background factor I found seventeen or fourteen point six five percent of my one hundred sixteen subjects had medical issues. After removing the high profile killers, professional athletes, and serial rapists, the total subjects is eighty five, my count drops to fifteen, but the percentage climbs to seventeen point six four percent, an increase of two point nine nine percent.

That makes four for four with higher results for the multiple murderers.

The fifth of the background factors is mental health issues. For this background factor I found thirty or twenty five point eight six percent of my one hundred sixteen subjects had mental health issues. After removing the high profile killers, professional athletes, and serial rapists, the total subjects is eighty five, my count drops to twenty six, but the percentage climbs to thirty point five eight percent, an increase of four point seven two percent.

That makes five for five with the higher results for the multiple murderers. At almost thirty one percent this is the highest percentage so far.

The sixth of the background factors is military service. This is another factor like homosexual tendencies, that isn't meant to imply that this group, military personal, should be viewed as negatively. However, when we look at the numbers, it is concerning. For this background factor I found nineteen or sixteen point three seven percent of my one hundred sixteen subjects had military service. After removing the high profile killers, professional athletes, and serial rapists, the total subjects is eighty five, my count drops to seventeen, but the percentage climbs to twenty point zero zero percent, an increase of three point six three percent.

That makes six for six with the higher results for the multiple murderers. At over twenty percent, that is a one in every five ratio.

I hope at some point in the future the military might adopt a policy like most law enforcement agencies have. When a police officer discharges a firearm in the pursuit, capture, or death of a subject he or she is required to participate in counseling.

It would be harder of course for military and can't be expected after every firearm discharge. But if a military personal has seen action it should be required of them to spend time at a designated program for a specified time period. For example, if they are on a two year tour, pull them out in twenty two or three months to spend the last thirty or sixty days decompressing and reacclimating back to society.

I know the military is not supposed to accept people with mental health issues, but it happens, whether by accident or need. Other's obtain their mental health issues from their experiences along with the knowledge, training, and unfortunately in some instances, the taste for killing.

The seventh of the background factors is paroled to kill again. For this background factor I found seven or six point zero three percent of my one hundred sixteen subjects had been paroled to kill again. After removing the high profile killers, professional athletes, and serial rapists, the total subjects is eighty five, my count stays at seven, but the percentage climbs to eight point two three percent.

I will not count this as seven for seven because this was obvious. You had to be a multiple murderer to be in this background factor. The one thing I would like to mention however, is this is the factor society has the most accountability and control over.

It is scary to think that of the eighty five multiple murderers in my study, seven were paroled to kill again. Almost ten percent. Think about that. That is on us.

The eighth of the background factors is physically abused. For this background factor I found seventeen or fourteen point six five percent of my one hundred sixteen subjects had been physically abused. After removing the high profile killers, professional athletes, and serial rapists, the total subjects is eighty five, my count drops to fifteen, but the percentage climbs to seventeen point six four percent, an increase of two point nine nine percent.

That makes seven for seven with the higher results for the multiple murderers.

The ninth of the background factors is sexually abused. For this background factor I found ten or eight point six two percent of my one hundred sixteen subjects had been sexually abused. After removing the high profile killers, professional athletes, and serial rapists, the total subjects is eighty five, my count drops to eight, but the percentage climbs to nine point four one percent, an increase of point seven nine percent.

That makes eight for eight with the higher results for the multiple murderers.

We also must consider this is the most under reported of the factors, especially for men, which my study is mainly made up of.

The tenth and final background factor is substance abusers. For this background factor I found sixteen or thirteen point seven nine percent of my one hundred sixteen subjects were substance abusers. After removing the high profile killers, professional athletes, and serial rapists, the total subjects is eighty five, my count drops to twelve, but the percentage climbs to fourteen point one one percent, an increase of point three two percent.

That makes nine for nine with the higher results for the multiple murderers. This was the smallest of the increases, but it was another increase.

What does this all mean? Let's move on to the conclusion and process this.

"We serial killers are your sons. We are your husbands. We are everywhere. And there will be more of your children dead tomorrow."

Ted Bundy

XXXXIX.

You have been given a lot of numbers to review and I am about to give you a few more to put things into a final perspective.

As a society we have been trying to establish a pattern or way to identify an individual before he becomes a mass, serial, or spree killer. I still can't give you an answer for that, but I can tell you it is more complex than we thought.

It's not just a matter of identifying who was abused or who has mental health issues. When this argument is made, someone will always state they knew someone who was abused and grew up fine. That is very true, but we have to realize we are all different, not just in body and spirit, but psychological makeup as well. What affects one person may not affect another, or have different results, etc. In other cases it takes two unique personalities to get together to create one personality that will kill. Had they not met they would never evolve into the killers they became.

I've always said it takes a perfect storm to create a multiple murderer, and now I have the evidence to back that up.

Of the eighty five multiple murderers in my study sixty four or seventy five point two nine percent had at least one background factor. Thirty eight of those sixty four or fifty nine point three seven percent had at least two background factors. Twenty of those sixty four or thirty one point two five percent had at least three background factors. Twelve of those sixty four or eighteen point seven five percent had at least four background factors. Six of those sixty four or nine point three seven percent had at least five background factors.

John Wayne Gacy had seven background factors and Arthur Shawcross had six background factors. These factors created a compulsion to kill that these individuals could not control and or understand. In John Gacy it took all seven factors to create him, in Arthur Shawcross it took all six, again each individual is different and needed more or less to evolve.

When you think that so many of these individuals fit into multiple background factors, it begs the question. How did no one notice or think they were seriously damaged people? This proves that there is a pattern, however it is different in each killer, but unique in that it needs multiple factors to evolve. I'm sure most members of our society do not fit into multiple background factors. We should be able to be more vigilant when it comes to monitoring people who start to fall into multiple categories.

Studies on the human brain are advancing day by day with so much still unexplored and unknown, hopefully one day the connection can be made on how outside factors affect it and alter it. Until then, no matter what we think of them, these killers are one of us. We all can kill, we all have fantasized about it on different levels. That does not make us evil. People fantasize about being victims as well. Yes they do, take the case of Armin Meiwes of Germany who posted an ad looking for someone willing to be killed and eaten. That ad was answered by Bernd Jurgen Armando Brandes who was in fact killed and eaten with his consent.

Does that make Bernd an evil man? He obviously had psychological issues, but was definitely not a bad person. When movies like Fifty Shades Of Grey rule the box office it is clear society fantasizes about being dominant and submissive. We don't like to admit to these things but we do.

To sum all of this up, I like to use a line from the movie Manhunter. F.B.I. agent Will Graham visits with Hannibal Lecter to get back into the mindset of catching a serial killer. Hannibal sensing this responds: "You came here to get a look at me, to get the old scent back again, didn't you? Do you know how you caught me, Will? The reason you caught me is that we're just alike. Do you understand? Smell yourself."

"These are the kids who never learned it's wrong to poke out a puppy's eyes."
Robert Ressler

XXXXX.

We have come to the end of The Long Dark Walk, but it is just the first step in a longer journey for me. I am at a point in my life where I need to do this full time. I have been working in the substance abuse field the last ten years and have become completely burned out.

With this book I hope to again conduct lectures and teach in the field, but at a much larger scale than before. I will also continue to write to multiple murderers throughout the world and hope to write another book on just one of them. I am undecided on who, but I want it to be one that is local and never had a book written on them.

I also plan to conduct some phone interviews with some murderers for a possible internet project. For now I have started a short story on serial killer John Wayne Gacy entitled The Clown That Became The Face Of Evil. This may be the start of a series of short stories on famous serial killers, or just a one shot, I haven't decided yet. I have so many ideas in my head and now have the confidence to follow through with them. At some point I would also like to donate my correspondences to a university as a private collection to be used for students majoring in either criminal justice or psychology.

But for now I would like to thank you for reading this book and I look forward to meeting some of you at my book signings. In closing I would like to leave you with a poem that serial killer Arthur Shawcross wrote for me. It seems fitting with everything we have discussed, but also because he was the first serial killer I would write.

SERIALS

Why is there a commonality to people like us, can it be our independence and self sufficiency that keeps our subsequent bizarre behavior distinguishable in violence of the rush.

With the severity of violence in the frenzy to execute anyone without remorse, without conscience thought – leaves one with memories in the silence.

The force we feel that no one finds or the unshakable belief and cumulative pitfalls, or the depression in combinations of severe pain of our kind.

I for one enunciate that I am much much more then stated by the people, the press, or the world in general.

If you see in us agitation, insanity, furor, excitability, delirium, violence or plain evil, then I suggest you look in the mirror.

By: Arthur J. Shawcross 9/1/95

INDEX

Ablow, Keith 85
Albright, Charles 119
Alcatraz Federal Penitentiary 100
Alphabet Killer 120
Anderson, Scott 123
Andrews, Ralph 54
Angelo, Richard 98
Anscombe, Roderick 85
Bar-Jonah, Nathaniel 57-58, 150
Bardo, Robert John 94, 96-97, 123
Beam, Alex 85
Berkowitz, David 8, 119, 120, 122
Bernardo, Paul 125
Bianchi, Kenneth 116, 120
Bittaker, Lawrence 17-18, 28
Bizanowicz, Michael 69-70
Blacks, Clyde 115
Blood Lust 17
Bolin, Oscar Ray 107
Bonin, William 18, 98-100, 108
Bowles, Gary Ray 86-88, 90, 158
Boyer, John Wayne 107

Brady, Ian 30-31
Bright, Larry 75
Brisbon, Henry 12
Brooks, David Owen 32
Brown, Alfred 25, 27
Brown, Debra 120
Brudos, Jerome 30
Bryant, Jason 76
Bundy, Carol 46
Bundy, Ted 5, 13, 85, 112, 188
Buono, Angelo 120
Buono, Christopher 120
Burris, Kristina 115
Bush, George W. 29
Butts, Vernon 99
California Medical Facility 101
Carignan, Harvey 100
Carlo, Phillip 10, 85
Carpenter, David 121
Chapman, Mark David 96-97
Chelmsford Public Library 58
Cherry, Raphel 40-41, 145

Clark, Bradfield 51, 121
Clark, Douglas 18, 46
Clark, Hadden 51-52, 121
Class Of Death 49
Claux, Nicolas 103
Coleman, Alton 120-121
College Guild 116
Columbia Correctional Institution 6
Columbine 92
Colvin, Dellmus 107
Compton, Veronica 120
Conahan, Daniel 101
Conner, Darion 66-67, 95, 145
Coonan, Peter 45
Cooper, Dana 123
Copeland, Joseph 115-116
Corcoran State Prison 101
Corll, Dean 32-33, 101-102
Cornelius, Tina Marie 48-49
Cornett, Natasha 31, 76
Corona, Juan 101-102
Corresponding With Serial Killers 52, 59
Cottingham, Richard 121
Couldn't Keep It To Myself 117

Counterpoint 15
Court TV 59, 63
Crafts, Richard 71
Crime Library 52, 59
Cullen, Charles 121
Curtis, Chad 86, 145
Dahmer, Jeffrey 6, 44, 65, 96, 131
Dardar, Ramsey 63-64, 145
Death Row Support Project 117
DeSalvo, Albert 40, 176
Dillon, Thomas 44
Dominique, Ronald 122
Douglas, John 12, 18
Downs, Diane 24
Drew, Carl 68
Druce, Joseph 69-70
Dushame, Peter 116
Etienne, Clifford 68-69
Evicci, Wilfred 69-70
Farley, Richard 49-50, 156
Fatal Attraction 55, 56
Ferguson, Colin 21, 102
Ferrell, Rod 123
Fish, Albert 96, 182

Flynn, William 82
Ford, Wayne Adam 107
Fowler, Raymond 82
Francois, Kendall 43-44
Fugate, Caril Ann 125
Fuller, Jamie 70
Furio, Jennifer 26, 83
Gacy, John 5-6, 12-13, 96, 102, 105, 186, 188
Gallego, Charlene 104, 125
Gallego, Gerald 104
Gates Of Janus 31
Gatti, Arturo 39
Gaynor, Alfred 61-62, 69-70
Gecht, Robin 104-105
Gein, Ed 96
Geoghan, John 69
Gilbert, Kristen 123
Gillis, Sean 123
Golden State Killer 97
Gore, David 25-26
Graham, David 92-93
Graham, Gwendolyn 124
Graham, Harrison 28-29, 44
Gray, Dana 91

Greineder, Dirk 40, 69-70
Hairston, James 116, 118, 138
Hammer, David Paul 115-117
Hansen, Robert 123-124
Heidnik, Gary 96
Heirens, William 9
Hendy, Cindy 124-125
Henley, Darryl 77, 145
Henley, Elmer 32-33
Hernandez, Aaron 69
Herzog, Loren 75
Highway Serial Killings Initiative 107-108
Hiles, Joe 100, 105-106
Hilton, Dave Jr. 39, 174
Hindley, Myra 31
Holman Correctional Facility 74
Holmes, James 123, 134
Homolka, Karla 125
Houston, Eric 91-92, 96, 144, 153
Howell, Karen 76
Hurd, Sam 126-127
I Can Make You Love Me 49-50
Illinois Department Of Corrections 9
Imprisoned Artists 50, 116

Ireland, Colin 126
Jablonski, Phillip 72
Jace, Michael 126
Jackson, Calvin 38-39, 61
Jesperson, Keith 46-47, 107
Johnson, Eddie 126-127
Jones, Bryan 35
Jones, Genene 76-78, 149
Jones, Jeremy 105
Journal Of Psychiatry & Law 19
Joyner, Anthony 61
Junta, Thomas 36
Kaczynski, Ted 109
Karnig, Ken 101, 107, 108-110
Kasper, Raymond 13
Kasso, Ricky 123
Kearney, Patrick 79
Keesee, Charity 123
Kemper, Edmund 96, 128
Kibbe, Roger 128
Killer Fiction 103
Killer Letters 36
Killer Speaks 88
King, Gary 17

Kinkel, Kip 48
Kokoraleis, Andrew 105
Kokoraleis, Thomas 105
Kraft, Randy 18, 34
Lake, Leonard 43
Lamb, Wally 117
Lane, Adam Leroy 107, 128-129
Lattime, Vance 82
Lawrence Eagle Tribune 52, 59
Leahy, Paul 70
Leavenworth Penitentiary 138
Lecter, Hannibal 187
Letters From Prison 83
Lewis, Ray 77
Lioy, Doreen 10
Lo, Wayne 36-37, 155, 168
London, Sondra 12, 103, 113
Long, Bobby Joe 21-22, 29
Lucas, Henry Lee 28-29
MacDonald Triad 3, 180-181
Maimoni, Thomas 14-16, 21, 23
Majors, Orville Lynn 57-59
Making Of A Serial Killer 103
Manhunter 187

Manley, Dexter 129-130
Manson, Charles 96
Marquette, Richard 38, 163
Maxwell, Bobby Joe 79-80
McBain, Michael 129
McCollom, Eugene 36, 40
McCowen, Christopher 69-70
McDermott, Michael 36, 69-70
McDonald, William 129
MCI-Cedar Junction 69
McNaughton Rule 5, 25
McVeigh, Timothy 36, 116
McWatters, Eugene 105-106
Medina, Brenda 117
Meiwes, Armin 186
Melrose Public Library 52
Mendenhall, Bruce 107-108
Michaud, Stephen 85
Miley, Gregory 99
Mind Of A Killer 41
Mindhunter 18
Misbegotten Son 7
Mississippi State Penitentiary 104
Mladinich, Robert 85

Monster In My Family 47
Moore, Melissa 47
Morrison, Tommy 130
Mortal Remains 68, 151
Mullin, Herbert 107-109
Mullins, Edward 76
Munro, James 99, 109
Murderabilia 8, 52, 87, 98-99, 101
Naposki, Eric 130-131
Nassar, George 69-70
Nebraska State Penitentiary 125
Neelley, Alvin 131
Neelley, Judith 131
New Bedford Highway Killer 70
Newton, Michael 113
Ng, Charles 43, 154
Nilsen, Dennis 131
Norris, Joel 22
Norris, Roy 17, 28
North Shore Community College 41, 49
North Shore Sunday 36, 49
Olsen, Jack 7
Olson, Clifford 23
Osborn Correctional Institution 20

Parker, Gerald 63

Parker, James 132

Parnell, Kenneth 135

Payne, Thomas 89-90, 147

Peterson, Scott 60-61, 152

Philpin, John 85

Pickton, Robert 54-55

Pike, Christa 30-31, 76

Press, Margaret 15

Prince, Cleophus 34-35

Pros And Cons 77

Rabbitt, Dennis 63-64

Rader, Dennis 96

Ramirez, Richard 9-11, 24, 62, 170

Ramsey, Evan 132-133

Ramsland, Katherine 58

Randall, Patrick 82

Ray, Cynthia 41-42

Ray, David Parker 124

Ray, Glenda Jean 124

Ressler, Robert 12, 66, 113, 191

Rhoades, Robert 107, 134

Ridgway, Gary Leon 103

Rifkin, Joel 21, 102

Risner, Joseph 76

Rissell, Monte Ralph 65-66

Riva, James 110

Rivera, Vincent 113

Rizzo, Todd 65

Rogers, Dayton Leroy 17

Rogers, Glen 110-111

Rogers, Richard 36, 134

Rolling, Danny 103

Rosen, Fred 85

Ross, Michael 19-20, 65, 88

Routier, Darlie 134-136

Rule, Ann 85

Russell, George 111

Salem Citizens' Police Academy 13

Salem Public Library 5

Sampson, Gary 36, 72-73, 148

San Quentin State Prison 17-18, 137

Sanders, Kregg 12, 99, 113

Say You Love Satan 123

Scammell, Henry 68

Scarver, Christopher 6

Schaefer, Gerald 103, 112-113

Schlichter, Art 80-81, 145

Seda, Heriberto 72-73
Sells, Tommy Lynn 82
Serial Killer Letters 26
Serial Killers: The Growing Menace 22
Serial Killers Of Literature And Film 49
Sharpe, Richard 36
Shattered Silence 47
Shawcross, Arthur 6-8, 119, 186, 190
Shermantine, Wesley 74-75, 85
Simpson, O.J. 110
Smart, Pamela 82-83, 117
Smith, Robert Benjamin 113
Smith, Susan 49, 135-136
Son of Sam Law 8
Sosa, Che 69-70
Southern Ohio Correctional Facility 121
Souza-Baranowski Correctional Center 69
Speck, Richard 100, 113
Spreitzer, Edward 105
Stano, Gerald 112-114
Stanton, Rick 99
Starkweather, Charles 125
Stayner, Cary 135-136
Strohmeyer, Jeremy 136
Sturgill, Crystal 76

Sullivan Correctional Facility 119-120
Surratt, Edward 107
Sutcliffe, Peter 45-46
Tavares, Daniel 69-70
Ten Most Wanted List 38, 87, 110, 121
Terry, Michael 94
Thomas, Michael 117
Tinning, Marybeth 136, 140
Toole, Ottis 29
Trawick, Jack 74-75
True Crime Book Group 58
True Vampires 103
Trump, Donald 92
Tulloch, Robert 132
Tully, Richard 117-118
Turvey, Brent 40
Unlikely Case Of Albert DeSalvo 40
Unsolved Mysteries 14
VICAP 107
Wallace, Henry Louis 52
Warmus, Carolyn 55-56
Waterfield, Fred 26
Weaver, Francis 58, 137
Weaver, Ward III 58, 137
Weaver, Ward Jr. 58, 107, 137

Webb, Emanuel 83-84

Whitman, Charles 113

Williams, Stanley "Tookie" 137

Williams, Wayne 137-138

Wilson, John Wesley 94-96

Wood, Catherine 124

Wood, James 116, 138

Woodfield, Randall 23-24, 33

Wuornos, Aileen 132, 138-139, 171

Yancy, Dennis Roy 124

Yates, Andrea 49

Yates, Robert Lee 51, 53

Zamora, Diane 92

Zodiac Killer 121

ABOUT THE AUTHOR

John Olszewski was born and raised in the historic city of Salem, Massachusetts. From a young age he became fascinated with true crime. This led to a lifelong journey to reach this pinnacle. Along the way John received degrees in Criminal Justice, Behavioral Science, and Counseling Psychology. He would work in the correctional system, lecture circuit, and always maintain ties to the world's most infamous murderers.

This debut novel is the first of what he hopes to be many. He is currently at work on a short story on serial killer John Wayne Gacy entitled The Clown That Became The Face Of Evil. John welcomes email at SKpsychevaluator@aol.com.